12

Demco, Inc. 38-293

American Library Association
Chicago and London 1998

Project editor: Joan McLaughlin

Text design: Dianne M. Rooney

Composition in Caslon 3 and Caslon 540 using QuarkXpress 3.32 by the dotted i

Printed on 50-pound Victor Offset, a pH-neutral stock, and bound in 10-point coated cover stock by Victor Graphics

The paper used in this publication meets the minimum requirements of American National Standard for Information Sciences—Permanence of Paper for Printed Library Materials, ANSI Z39.48-1992. ∞

Library of Congress Cataloging-in-Publication Data

Wilson, Thomas C. (Thomas Carl), 1958–
    Systems librarianship / Thomas C. Wilson.
        p.   cm.
    Includes bibliographical references (p.   ) and index.
    ISBN 0-8389-0740-7
      1. Libraries—Data processing—Management.   2. Libraries—United States—Data processing—Management.   I. Title.
Z678.9.W55   1998
025'.00285—dc21
                          98-23105

Printed in the United States of America.

03 02 01 00 99   5 4 3 2 1

To

Ginny,
Bill,
Karl,
and
Paul,

all who left the party
much too soon!

CONTENTS

PREFACE

OVER THE PAST TWENTY YEARS OR SO, I HAVE HAD A VARIETY OF interactions with computers and automation, from my first programming class to running an online search service, developing training materials, designing networks, and managing a large systems department in an academic library. With all of this experience, I have come to see the very real value of professionals who are well versed in technology, management, and people skills, no matter what academic discipline they pursued. As I have found my current home in library systems work, it is my hope that in some way I can contribute to the continuing development of systems librarians who offer these critical sets of skills.

Moreover, there is a dearth of written material on the topic of systems librarianship. Many articles and books talk about subjects that are related to systems work or that set computing in a library context. Recently several authors published pieces that attempt to describe what people in the role of systems librarian actually do (Martin 1988; Muirhead 1994c) or how systems departments are organized (Muir 1995). Perhaps part of the lack of materials relates to the still developing role of systems librarians. No one would argue that libraries have not seen a significant rise in the use of computing and related technologies. Typically roles evolve over long periods of time, without the benefit of any clear strategy. Indeed, while systems librarians have existed in one form or another since the late 1950s, now we see increasing numbers of these types of positions, both formal and informal.

John Head (1993, xi) asks in his introduction to a practical guide to automation, "Is there even the remotest excuse for another book about library automation?" It is with some trepidation that I offer this text, but my focus is not strictly on automation—partly because such a work would quickly become dated. Rather, my goal is to provide an assessment of what systems librarianship is and can be, to outline in broad strokes the type of training that is needed for people to fill these positions, and to illustrate what I believe to be important challenges for libraries—and systems librarians—in computing and networking. In the process I will venture into prescriptive territory because I believe librarianship needs more than just descriptive materials about systems roles—we must look at *why* we do some things and why we perhaps should not do others.

My recent work has been in a large academic library, and good or bad, my perspective is colored by that experience. I have, however, worked in a variety of other environments, both inside and outside of libraries. Furthermore, I have consulted for a variety of businesses on technology issues. I also bring to this project experiences from an array of other disciplines and career paths, ranging from music to construction to ancient history. All these experiences temper my interpretations of librarianship and technology and the challenges we face. They also provide material for a variety of analogies.

It is only fair to admit at the start that I strongly believe in the need for systems librarians in library organizations (and in the functions they perform in many other organizations). I do not think, nor have I seen demonstrated, that central information technology management and support necessarily displaces creativity, efficiency, and innovation. I believe these qualities stem instead from the personalities both of individuals and organizations. I do, however, see that there are no perfect solutions nor one right answer for any problem, and I will remind the reader of that throughout this work.

Aspiring systems librarians will find substantive information about the specialty in these pages. My ideas will also inform administrators and managers who share accountability for library systems as well as practicing systems librarians who want to step back and look at the big picture.

ACKNOWLEDGMENTS

I AM DEEPLY INDEBTED TO MANY INDIVIDUALS FOR THEIR SUPPORT in librarianship and for the preparation of this book. First to Jim Rucker who more than anyone influenced me to become a librarian through the demonstration of its art and science. Then to Robin Downes, Dana Rooks, and Charles Bailey who provided the opportunity for me to learn firsthand the contents of this book and the support to bring it to fruition. To all past and present staff in our systems department who have made the journey exciting and productive, I am grateful: Steve Bonario, Harvey Brauner, Matt Cameron, Daniel Castellanos, Guadalupe García, Vernon Kahanek, Rick Labs, Hien Le, José Marinero, Beth Martin, Dat Nguyen, Sheetal Sheth, Rob Spragg, Ann Thornton, and Wei Wu. I greatly appreciate the review and comments of Milton Wolf, Barbra Higginbotham, Pat Ensor, Kate Wakefield, and Liz Lane Lawley; whatever errors or difficult passages remain are solely my responsibility. For encouragement and support, I thank Patrick Hogan from ALA Editions who pursued the idea of a book until I yielded. And I am most grateful to Caryn and Nichole Wilson for their love and support and the giving of many weekends. I am a truly fortunate man.

1

Toward a Philosophy of Systems Librarianship

A question formed upon stilled lips is passed on but never asked.

—Cowboy Junkies,
Something More Besides You

Despite the significant investments libraries have made in information technology, not much has been written about the people who manage these resources within library organizations. Perhaps this reflects the fact that libraries have dealt with technology as an additive process, calling on existing staff to meet these new needs in combination with their other responsibilities. The literature that does exist consists of limited surveys, opinion pieces, and calls to action. Most of the material focuses on duties related to integrated library systems (e.g., selection, requests for proposals [RFPs], management, and training), systems analysis, and incorporating microcomputers and related technology into library operations. A related body of writing consists of general technical information aimed at the computer literacy of all librarians, not just technology specialists.

In one form or another systems librarians have existed for many years. They have been called by a number of different titles (e.g., Automation Librarian, Computer Services Librarian, or Technology

Librarian), have served in a variety of departments, and have performed a wide array of duties. Both history and current practice indicate wide variation in the field, strong commitments to local arrangements, and a lack of functional standards. To encourage new recruits for systems librarianship and to inform others in the profession, a review of the nature of systems work in libraries, the services provided by this professional specialty, and the needs of systems staff is needed.

Toward a Philosophy

The term "philosophy" suggests a variety of definitions. Here it can be taken to mean a basic theory or viewpoint—an inquiry based on logical reasoning rather than on empirical methods. Philosophy also implies a system of values by which one lives, a critique and analysis of fundamental beliefs. To explore a philosophy of systems librarianship, one must first define what systems librarianship is. Several authors have already made the attempt:

> The systems librarian is the middleman, the go-between of the supplier and user: priest-like interpreter of the mysteries; hippy-like dealer in good vibes. (Dunsire 1994, 69)

> [Systems librarians are] the people who identify the needs of the library for automated systems, cause these systems to be implemented, and analyze the operations of the library. (Martin 1988, 57)

> A careful examination of [systems librarian job advertisements] reveals a fuzzy definition of the duties of the position. Anything related to computers may be mentioned. (Chu 1990, 91)

> [The systems librarian is] Maintainer, Interpreter, Trainer, Enabler, Liaison, and Advisor. (Lynch 1994, 40)

> The primary responsibilities of an Automation Librarian . . . include the following: 1) developing original applications; 2) troubleshooting; 3) software evaluation; 4) hardware/software monitoring, main-

tenance, and upgrading; 5) data protection; 6) staff training; 7) system documentation; and 8) negotiation and communication.

(White 1990, 257)

So what's it like being a systems librarian? Busy.

(Schuyler 1994, 98)

Certainly in most settings the definition varies considerably. For some, systems librarians are responsible for training staff in computer applications, such as components of an integrated system or word processing. For others, they function as the liaisons with the "real" computer people, whether in a city data processing department, a university information technology division, or an in-house unit of technicians. In some environments, systems librarians are the "computer people" as well. And in many cases, systems librarians wear all of these hats.

Perhaps it would also be useful to outline what a systems librarian *is not:*

> online searcher
>
> computer user
>
> software hack
>
> power user
>
> Internet user
>
> Online Computer Library Center (OCLC) guru
>
> information technology policy maven
>
> information scientist
>
> researcher

While a systems librarian might possess any or all of these skills, they are not the sole purview of these specialists. Any librarian could, in fact should, possess some of these skills. Indeed, many of them are included in the basic training of all librarians. But none of them individually constitutes a definition of what a systems librarian is or does in relation to other librarians or to the profession in general. Viewing systems librarianship from the perspective of "those who use computers" or those who know something about computers has serious implications for the definition of all specializations within libraries and for the preserve and continuing education of all librarians. (See Chapter 3, "The Education of a Systems Librarian.")

Approaching systems librarianship in terms of what it is and is not, however, generates definitions that are solely descriptive. The answers simply reflect what people in these positions do or the functions they provide. One can address the issue slightly different to achieve a broader perspective: why have a systems librarian position? This question suggests that something exists a bit deeper in the nature of systems librarianship and the development and use of technology in libraries.

Libraries encompass a variety of tasks, resources, services, relationships, and functions. For some areas of librarianship there are clear boundaries of responsibility and spheres of influence. While there is always room for local interpretation and variance, there is wide agreement on what constitutes, for example, an acquisitions librarian, a reference librarian, or a preservation officer. Not so with systems librarians. Furthermore, despite its lengthy existence, systems librarianship has not enjoyed the same status or recognition as have other areas of librarianship (Martin 1988). This is probably related to the lack of understanding of what specifically constitutes systems librarianship, the overlap between many of the responsibilities of systems librarians and those of members of other professions (or professional specialties within librarianship), and the unarticulated uniqueness of this subfield. Some have even questioned the appropriateness of having librarians performing systems responsibilities, arguing that other technical staff should be employed for these duties.

As libraries have become increasingly automated, the existence of some type of systems librarian has become more common. With librarians moving to second- and third-generation systems and integrating scores of electronic resources for patron access, the need for systems personnel has become commonplace. At the same time, much has been written in the popular computing, management, and library press about the need to avoid the negative aspects of centralized control of computing resources, like those experienced in organizations served by data processing departments running large mainframes (Drake 1986; Jaffe 1991; Medina 1983; Mitchell 1994). The rise of microcomputers has often been cited as a user's tool for freedom from misguided, noncommunicative "control freaks" employed in computing departments. Alley graphically presents this image:

A familiar scene from the period was the librarian on bended knee in the computer center director's office trying desperately to get a project approved or moved up in the queue. The center director had the ultimate say and had complete control over institutional computing. It was a difficult battle for the librarian, and because of it, libraries rarely got their fair share of the total computing time available. Fortunately, the personal computer arrived in the nick of time and changed all that. (Alley 1991, 80–81)

In attempting to identify and articulate the conceptual under-pinnings of a professional specialization, an author risks sounding trivial or trite. In proposing a broad-based definition and explication of what systems librarians are and should be, the goal is not to draw lines in the sand and create barriers or fiefdoms within librarian-ship—there are enough of those already. Instead, I propose to outline those areas of expertise and responsibility—and therefore training and education—that normally fall within the scope of systems librar-ianship and to discuss the unique blend of skills, attitudes, ap-proaches, and insights that a person trained both in librarianship and computing can offer. The intent is not to diminish other roles, but to celebrate the partnerships that are possible.

A Brief History of Computing in Libraries

To understand what systems librarians can be, it is instructive to consider what librarians and others involved in library automation have accomplished to date. From the development of the Machine-Readable Cataloging (MARC) standard; the establishment of the Ohio College Library Center; the trailblazing efforts of Florida At-lantic University, Northwestern University, and Stanford University; and the creation of the Medline and ERIC databases, libraries have been active in technological projects for more than thirty years. Pre-dating these efforts and continuing to the present, librarians have a rich history of incorporating mechanical and electronic devices into library services (Grosch 1995; Kent 1986; Salmon 1975).

It is worth noting that the early experiments with computing oc-curred at a time when most of the profession was less than certain of the usefulness of automation projects (Wasserman 1965). These investigations were also made in a computing era in which the vision necessary to imagine the eventual utility of the projects required a leap of faith. After all, seeing beyond punch cards to interactive applications, or conceptually moving from multimillion-dollar annual computing budgets to off-the-shelf automation packages in the hundreds of dollars was difficult in the 1960s.

In fact, libraries have been involved in the deployment of technology since their inception. The use of storage media—whether papyrus, clay, or CD-ROM—is a deployment of technology, as are various techniques for organizing and retrieving materials. Libraries represent a merger and an evolution of multiple technologies. More recently, libraries have used computing to provide efficient storage and retrieval of materials, share cataloging information, identify remotely held items, inventory collections, deliver information to the requestor, distribute important data, and further many other functions and goals (Salmon 1975).

At the heart of these activities has been some person or persons who guided the application or development of specific technologies that address library needs. In many cases, projects involved professionals from a variety of backgrounds. Systems analysts and programmers from data processing units along with catalogers and technical services librarians combined their respective talents and perspectives to develop systems that provided more functionality than their manual counterparts. The creation of the MARC record, the bibliographic utilities, and interlibrary loan protocols are examples of librarians participating in the development and use of technologies to improve library efficiency and services.

From the 1950s through the early 1980s, most of the emphasis in deploying computing technology in libraries focused on internal operations, such as the identification and acquisition of materials and inventory management (i.e., circulation). In the mid-1970s with the growth of online subject-specific databases, large centralized time-share systems began to be used to distribute access to libraries and businesses. Mediated online searching became popular, usually offered in the reference department. As multiple technologies converged (e.g., microcomputers and compact discs) and as patrons began to feel comfortable performing their own searches, a large library market developed for CD-ROM databases.

The rise of microcomputers and business software (e.g., word processing, spreadsheets, presentation software), the availability of online catalogs for local holdings, and the increase in database searching (both online and CD-ROM) led to a major shift in emphasis for computing in libraries. Before, most computing was found behind the scenes; as these newer technologies were deployed in many libraries, computing became much more visible.

During the mid-1980s local area networking became viable for many organizations. Libraries began to enjoy the same benefits as businesses, making a variety of resources available through networks (e.g., subject-specific databases, catalogs, productivity software, etc.). By the late 1980s and early 1990s, libraries sometimes far exceeded the business community in the deployment of networking, integrating multiple technologies to provide customized information services for their users.

As a backdrop for all this development, in the 1960s what is now called the Internet began evolving. It did not exist much beyond certain segments of the academic, research, and military communities until the early 1990s, at which point popular services, such as Gopher and the World Wide Web (WWW), captured the attention of many. These later examples have pushed library computing even more into the public eye to such an extent that many libraries are expected to provide significant amounts of free public access to the Internet.

Identifiable Trends and Consequences

Any historical interpretation or analysis runs the risk of suggesting the existence of trends that are cleaner in concept than they were in reality. Nonetheless, it is fair to say that library computing projects first focused on automating backroom functions. This notion, however, can lead to some confusion: it was first necessary to create an infrastructure from which other applications could grow, hence the work on issues such as MARC records.

The widely held opinion that behind-the-scenes operations were automated first because they were the easiest or most straightforward is misguided. One could argue that some of these functions still remain challenging to automate, precisely because they are complex. These backroom library services were chosen first because many of them mirrored functions that business was also struggling to automate, they appeared to have the greatest likelihood of payoff, and the people employed in these areas of the libraries were often thought of as "technical" staff.

As libraries' options and success rates increased and spread, attention began to focus on other areas of operations and services. Online catalogs became a major theme in library automation in the late 1970s and early 1980s. Other applications also received attention: reference database searching, administrative functions such as decision support and budget analysis, and general office automation activities such as word processing. The technological infusion within organizations was also furthered by the development and availability of microcomputers.

This shift in interest was significant in two respects. First, it represented a move from internal operations to services that directly affected library patrons and were visible to library constituencies. Second, these new automation efforts involved library departments that previously were able to ignore the projects that were under way. The manner in which these new endeavors played themselves out determined to a large degree the nature of systems librarianship. The traditional divisions in libraries, public and technical services, also influenced the development of systems librarianship, in terms of responsibilities, skills, and image. This way of seeing the world has also affected the organization and reporting structure of library systems offices.

Image and Definition of Technical Staff

The library community attributes to systems librarians some of the same traits ascribed to catalogers: focused on details, unable to be serendipitous, and policy- or rule-bound. The engineer-technician image enters into this view as well. The common perception of people who work with computers, the product of years of portrayals, adds to the confusion: the white-coated laboratory elites of the past have become the pocket-protector nerds of today, so inward-looking that they cannot be trusted with mission-critical operations because they know too much and have too much control. Assuming that all systems librarians miss the forest for the trees is no different from asserting that all reference librarians are more concerned with the sharpness of golf pencils than with the accuracy of answers. Systems librarians can also engender contempt from their computing industry colleagues for a lack of technical understanding and experience. In fact, systems librarians are often caught in the middle of two "industries," neither of which completely embraces them. To a large degree, they function as outsiders.

Despite the negative associations attributed to people in technical positions, library systems staff have a rich and proud history that has had great impact on the mission and operations of libraries of all types. These accomplishments have not come without significant challenges, both locally and across the profession. Given the somewhat checkered past of systems librarianship, it might be useful to outline the general role of the library technical staff. This area of inquiry presents a challenge, because the definition of technical work in libraries has traditionally stemmed from the Greek and Latin meanings of "technical": applying some specialized art, skill, or technique. In most cases, technical work of this type has been performed in acquisitions, cataloging, and serials units, thus the "technical services" moniker. Randall (1940, 1) referred to these skills as "the secrets of the craft."

It is not surprising then that when computing, a "technical" activity, was introduced into many libraries, the responsibility for it became part of these "technical" units. (The one common variance from this model was in the automation of circulation units with stand-alone systems.) In a paper on technology competencies for technical services, Henderson (1983) notes the derision over the years of technical services activities and their more recent rise in standing in part owing to the use of technology. She outlines a variety of computer competencies in terms of workflow processes, resources accessed, and tools employed, and characterizes these as layers on top of other more traditional skills and responsibilities.

Beyond this first definition of "technical" (any specialized skill) lies a second, encompassing not only very specific sets of skills, but also an entire scientific development (computing technology) and process application (systems analysis and design). With these definitional differences in mind, it is worth noting that nothing in the general preparation of librarians from previous generations (other than familiarity with the function being automated) would have made a cataloger any more qualified to do systems work than a reference librarian would have been.

At this point the reader may be thinking that semantics has no relevance to systems librarianship. Quite the contrary: the language one uses to describe the world reflects one's understanding of and underlying beliefs about it. More directly to the point of systems librarianship, current practices and organizational schemes are as they are precisely because of these definitions and understandings. For the individual considering systems librarianship, it is worth knowing the history; for those wishing to shape the future of systems librarianship, it is imperative to understand the factors that created this history.

What Is a Systems Librarian, Really?

With that review in mind, one can examine in more detail the nature of systems librarianship. The literature on systems librarianship indicates that the people in these positions perform many duties, ranging from training to interfacing with information technology centers to serving on the reference desk (Chu 1990; Martin 1988; Muir 1995; Muirhead 1994c). In short, a systems librarian is a specialist, like an acquisitions librarian, reference librarian, or interlibrary loan librarian. Just as the people in these other specialties receive focused preservice training and develop on-the-job expertise in their respective areas, systems librarians acquire the knowledge and skill levels they need through a variety of opportunities.

In an ideal environment, systems librarians would have a solid understanding of the operations of most, if not all, units within libraries, in addition to understanding systems work. In reality, systems librarians will have reasonable knowledge of some areas of libraries and acquire the needed details of others along the way. In the most constructive settings, this circumstance leads to a professional interdependence among library staff.

Systems librarianship, however, is not solely comprised of library knowledge. To be an effective systems librarian, one must also possess knowledge of library automation, computing, and networking. On the surface, it may appear that these demands are too disparate and no one could possibly be expected to function adequately in both arenas (i.e., libraries and computing). Muirhead (1994c) and others have indicated the stress experienced by systems librarians precisely because the expectation is that these people will be fluent in a wide variety of issues in both professional communities. Chu (1990, 91) notes that systems positions ". . . often do not lend themselves to the talents of a single person."

The irony, as Muirhead notes, is twofold. First, systems librarians tend to flourish in this environment and find satisfaction from the very things that cause stress (1994c, 34). And second, these positions intriguingly combine sets of contradictions: "the world of humans and the world of machines"; "a low group profile externally and nationally and yet much influence internally"; "on the periphery of library work, yet indispensible [sic] for the day-to-day operation of the most basic services"; "a specialism with no real homogeneity or uniformity in terms of the job content, and in which the postholder can expect to find him/herself cast in a variety of roles—librarian, technician, computer professional, manager, educator"; "the glamour, the high drama, and the stress of crisis situations, and the tedium of system error reports or ongoing minor hardware faults" (Muirhead 1993, 124).

To understand the nature of systems librarianship, it is helpful to contrast it with other types of librarianship, other computing professionals, and other serious computer users. The goal is to provide an outline of who these people are and what responsibilities they carry, not to present them all as martyrs, even though at times those in this specialty may wish to be viewed as such.

In Contrast to Other Librarians

Analogies are always limited in their application; thus it is with some concern that I offer one for systems librarianship. As mentioned previously, systems librarians are similar to other specialists in libraries because they bring a given set of skills to the table and offer certain perspectives to an organization. Systems librarians specifically concentrate on supporting library operations through the application of technologies.

Some would suggest that the roles they play would best be served by other managers within an organization. For some, systems librarians are not needed because in their minds the best way to manage computing within an organization is to distribute the responsibility to each department. Systems librarians, however, are not all that different from acquisitions/collection development librarians in the following manner: just as acquisitions librarians may coordinate the activities of many subject selectors or collection development librarians may integrate the suggestions of multiple reference librarians, faculty, or general users into their decisions, systems librarians coordinate the effective use of technology throughout the organization regardless of the department concerned. They seek to manage the organizational technological resources in a manner that best serves all departments within a library.

In terms of knowledge and skill about other library units, given that many of the people currently in systems positions have come from other departments, this expertise may already be present. In this regard, the expectations of systems librarians are not different from those of other librarians, particularly with the recent trends in job sharing, position rotations, and interdepartmental cross-training. The one area in which there is, or should be, a difference is in the level of expertise in dealing with and managing computing and networking. All librarians, including systems librarians, need to use computers to some degree to perform their duties. The level of knowledge and responsibility, however, is much higher for the systems librarian in this case. Certainly, systems librarians do not have a corner on computing knowledge, but they can be in the best position to see the issues that relate to the overall implementation and management of information technology resources within the organization. Given this perspective, they have a duty to be intimately familiar with the technology, both that which is currently employed and that which is potentially useful; the people who use it throughout the organization; and the applications and services in use and available in the market.

This level of responsibility does not imply that systems librarians are the only ones who "do technology"; in fact, these positions exist so that *others* can "do technology." Through effective implementation, maintenance, and training, systems librarians ensure that the investment that an organization has made in technology remains productive and useful. How exactly this role plays itself out varies from library to library, as it should.

In Contrast to Computer Scientists/Management Information Systems (MIS) Specialists

Many titles are given to positions in industry that require computer science or management information systems (MIS) degrees, or other related background: system analyst, network administrator, computer programmer, system design specialist, system administrator, software support analyst, hardware engineer, etc. These titles reflect a general tendency in computing to specialize. The breadth of knowledge to understand all of computing, not to mention networking, is overwhelming. Computing is certainly not one thing. The response in many cases, particularly in large organizations, is to create subspecialties within computing. For example, an information technology unit in a medium-sized organization (e.g., 300 employees) might employ ten individuals to cover the areas of computing and networking in use within the business:

Position Title	*Number of Positions*
Manager	1
Programmer/Analyst 1	2
Programmer/Analyst 2	1
Hardware Support Technician	3
Software Support Specialist	1
Desktop Support Manager/Trainer	1
Network Administrator	1

In this example, six technical specialties are identified: systems analysis, programming, hardware, software, training, and network administration. In each case, except systems analysis and programming, different individuals are responsible for these areas. Although this example is not taken from a particular workplace, it represents the way computing and networking are handled in many organizations.

In libraries, particularly small and medium-sized ones, however, a more common approach is to have one or a small number of people handling a variety of subspecialties (Muir 1995; Muirhead 1994a; Muirhead 1994b). Systems librarians are called on to be fluent in many different aspects of computing and networking. Thus, they are expected to possess a wide-ranging array of knowledge and skill in both library and computing operations at significant depths.

In Contrast to Power Users

For the sake of this discussion, a power user is defined as someone who has substantial experience with a particular set of applications that demand high levels of computing power. In many circumstances, such users are valuable assets to organizations. They provide direct services in the areas in which they are expert, and they can provide additional support for other users in co-located areas that need assistance with applications or have questions about computing. They frequently serve as advocates for technology implementation within an organization.

Many systems librarians may have been power users who developed into system managers. This experience is common in this profession. As a general rule, however, there is a difference between a power user and a systems librarian. Power users may become systems librarians, but there are specific areas in which they will need to develop.

Power users frequently are focused on particular technologies or applications, as opposed to the wide array of options that an organization may need to implement. Favoritism toward specific technologies can mislead power users and their organizations.

Systems librarianship demands broad and deep technical expertise and experience with many relevant technologies. Sometimes power users may desire computing power for power's sake, a diversion that can misdirect institutional resources. Systems librarians must learn to match the level of computational power with the need of a particular application in light of overall technology defusion within an organization.

Power users may tend to focus on technologies that advance only certain areas of the library. For an organization to benefit widely from the deployment of information technology, all units must receive attention to their respective needs. Systems librarians need to view the entire enterprise from a total resource management perspective; systems work is more than just a few fancy computers or a really cool Web presence.

A View from the Field

What specifically constitutes the responsibilities of a systems librarian? According to Muirhead's survey of UK librarians, some common elements are: planning and implementing a library system (including upgrading), system maintenance (including operations, programming, hardware maintenance, staff and user documentation and training, management information, and budget), and other computing duties (including office automation, CD-ROM, microcomputer applications, network management, theater automation, security systems, and others). He notes that the majority of respondents also perform a variety of noninformation technology duties, such as information desk service, shelving, cataloging, and collection development, among others (Muirhead 1994c, 6–11).

Muir (1995) notes in his survey of the Association of Research Libraries (ARL) members that an expansion of responsibilities was a common theme in systems offices between the years 1990 and 1994. Responsibilities include not only the traditional library management system, but also bibliographic utility equipment, staff and public microcomputers and peripherals, training, CD-ROM services, Internet/Gopher/Web, mainframe maintenance, local and remote database access, Campus-Wide Information Systems (CWIS), networking, microcomputer repair, and workstation design.

A review of systems position announcements advertised between July 1996 and October 1997 includes the following lengthy and diverse set of responsibilities:

Knowledge of and experience with specific technologies:

> academic information systems
> applications software (e-mail, word processing, groupware)
> audiovisual technologies
> bibliographic database software and applications
> bibliographic utilities
> CD-ROM
> client server, distributed systems, and heterogeneous
>   computing
> computer languages/environments (PL/1, 4GL, DCL,
>   JCL, Pick, SQL, Java, Java Script, SAS)
> database creation, publishing, and management
> database vendor interfaces
> DECNet
> dial-in services and technologies
> document delivery services and technologies
> electronic classrooms
> electronic library infrastructure
> file transfer protocols
> financial systems
> geographic information systems
> imaging technologies
> instructional technology
> Internet (WWW, Gopher, Telnet/TN3270, CGI)
> local area network (LAN) administration
> locally mounted databases (integrated library system
>   [ILS] and separate)
> log analysis tools

mainframe library applications

multimedia applications, authoring, and image database design

network infrastructure and environments

operating systems (Unix, Solaris, OpenVMS, VM, CICS, TSO, Mac OS, Windows)

personal computers

relational databases

retrieval tools

security and authentication technologies

Standard Generalized Markup Language (SGML) and Hypertext Markup Language (HTML)

wide area network (WAN) technologies

Z39.50

Other knowledge and experience:

Certified NetWare Engineer

computer design and repair

current information technology trends

data processing

database loads

determining and writing specifications

evaluation of new hardware and software

grant writing

hardware, software, network development

history of library information technology

license negotiation

Microsoft Certified System Engineer

national standards

operations

project management

proposal writing

requirements analysis

statistics

system installation

systems development methodologies

USMARC format

Technical management:

coordinate library automation with university-wide computing initiatives

develop policies

liaison between library and other libraries, computer analysts, telecommunication analysts, data control operations, and database providers

liaison with consortia

liaison with OCLC

long-range planning

monitor expenses

plan, develop, organize, staff, budget, evaluate

purchase equipment and supplies

recommend new technologies, initiatives, and services

restructure services and units

supervise technical staff

technological advice

Technical support:

beta testing

documentation and training

help desk and telephone support

routine and customized reports

system testing

technical writing

translate computer and library jargon

Working habits, attitudes, and environments:

able to prioritize

accommodate emergencies

   aptitude for learning new technology

   collaboration

   courtesy under pressure

   creative leadership and direction

   customer service

   excellent written, oral, and electronic
      communication skills

   interdependent relationships

   interpersonal skills

   meeting deadlines

   multitask

   organizational skills

   quality assurance

   resource sharing

   team-oriented

   user-responsiveness

   work under pressure

It would seem that the organizations employing systems librarians expect them to possess a wide array of skills. Each of these libraries will require a slightly variant set of responsibilities just as one would expect for catalogers or reference librarians. It is important to recognize that, particularly in larger settings, many of these duties may be overseen by a systems librarian, while actually being carried out by nonlibrarian staff (e.g., programmers, support specialists, analysts, network managers, etc.).

The Doing versus the Managing

A digression seems appropriate at this point. In the previous sections, I have outlined the involvement of systems librarians in specific areas. There are those in the profession who would suggest that someone with a master's degree should not attempt to do this level of technical work. This opinion stems from three beliefs: such work is beneath someone with high-level training and education, librarians are managers not doers, and specific tasks should be matched to appropriate position classifications to minimize the cost of performing them. These three statements warrant further examination for they illustrate challenges facing libraries with regard to systems work and attitudes toward it.

Technical Work Is beneath Me

To address the first statement, technical work is beneath someone with high-level training and education, it is necessary to note the general mission of libraries. In its simplest form, the mission statement for all libraries includes the provision of collections, access, and services to a constituency. Certainly, many complexities and nuances influence the interpretation of such a statement for each library in a fashion that reflects local needs, resources, and constraints. An attitude that suggests that librarians remain aloof from this central mission, however, has no place in a service profession.

Under the surface of this statement also appear two pragmatic misrepresentations. The first revolves around a notion of how work gets done. In any organization, there are times when procedures go as planned, and there are times when the unexpected occurs. For example, under normal circumstances, perhaps it makes sense for a librarian not to sweep the floor because someone else has that responsibility, but when that person is otherwise detained and a spill is interrupting service, "normal" no longer applies.

The second misrepresentation ignores the fact that many technical professions require significant advanced training and education. So, arguing that librarians are somehow exempt from this type of technical work because of superior education carries little weight in discussions with people outside the profession, and fosters contempt for the profession in general. Furthermore, defensive posturing in any profession frequently, if not always, devolves into meaningless, unproductive turf wars.

Every Librarian a Manager

A favorite image-boosting statement that all librarians are managers has received much airplay. On the surface, such a statement appears harmless and perhaps true. Beneath the surface, however, this statement suggests that librarians are, in contrast to the doers of things, hands-off, removed, and distant. Particularly with regard to technology, such an attitude does not serve the profession well. Those who just "read" about the technology, as opposed to those who use it, grasp it, and understand it, are destined to be controlled by it—not exactly a positive, forward-looking image of the profession.

Subtle differences in one's approach to management can easily lead to a misunderstanding of what one is managing. It has been popular at times in management theory to argue that a manager does not need to be intimately familiar with the process he or she is managing. Furthermore, to avoid the technocrats taking over, some would argue that the manager of technology in libraries should not be a technical person. While this argument has some validity, it confuses the person in the position with the position itself. There is no inherent reason to believe that all technically trained people cannot see the implications and limitations of technologies. In fact, having someone with a strong technical background bounded with a good dose of realism in his or her approach as a manager would be a significant advantage for any library. Concomitantly, there is also no reason to believe that having a well-defined position guarantees that it will be filled with a savvy technical manager.

Systems librarians, with their feet in two professions, must understand and have handled the technology to be prepared to manage it. They must continue to be willing to touch the technology in ways that benefit the staff and the users of libraries. Librarians, whether managers or not, must do what is necessary to get the job done. As libraries further and further depend on various technologies, it would be wise for all librarians to keep in mind the value of having individuals with ties to multiple disciplines involved in managing the lives of libraries.

Minimize the Cost

The third statement in regard to technical work, specific tasks should be matched to appropriate position classifications to minimize the cost of performing them, is a concise iteration of a basic goal in good management. The idea is to apply wisely the available resources in a fashion that accomplishes the objectives of the organization without unduly expending fiscal, human, or other resources —in other words, stewardship.

Good management suggests that employing a highly trained technical professional to clean monitor screens does not make economic sense. The assumption, however, is that there is someone else available to do the job, which may or may not be true. Given that systems librarian duties vary greatly from library to library, it is difficult to state with certainty what is reasonable in this regard. It is clear, however, that the extremes in attitude are neither becoming, nor productive, for librarianship. These extremes would be: "I don't do screens." on the one end and "Is your keyboard dirty, too?" on the other.

Perhaps the clearest way to state this point is to offer a set of questions for librarians to ask themselves at times when they are avoiding a task:

1. Am I not doing this task because I refuse to do it?
2. Am I not doing this task because I don't know how to do it?
3. Am I not doing this task because there is someone else more appropriate and available to do it?
4. Am I not doing this task because it does not fit with the mission of my library?
5. What am I doing to see that this task can be accomplished successfully when the need occurs again in the future?

The answers given to these questions will determine whether a problem exists and whether it is related to attitude, technical training, or management.

A New Specialty

Systems librarianship represents a blend of library science, computer operations, and management. Historically, this specialty arose out of existing library positions in response to technological advancements within libraries. It is now a bona fide segment of the profession. For more than thirty years, the contributions of people in these positions have defined the nature of the field.

2

Responsibilities and Roles of Systems Librarians

Sing in me, Muse, and through me tell the story. . . .
—Homer, *The Odyssey*

The breadth of skills and responsibilities that define the purview of systems librarians and grant them a professional identity has been outlined. Common areas of responsibility for systems librarians, however, should be explored in greater depth. These include: integrated system management; network design and management; server and host administration; desktop computing; training, documentation, and support; application development; planning and budget; specification and purchasing; technology exploration and evaluation; miscellaneous technology support; technical risk management; and communication and coordination. These technical areas are frequently combined with more general management responsibilities.

Common Systems Responsibilities in Detail

Integrated System Management

The most common duty by far for systems librarians is the management of an integrated library system, or some module of the system.

These systems that provide cataloging, acquisitions, serials, circulation, online catalog, reserves, interlibrary lending, and other information management components have been the major focus of library automation since the beginning. Thus, these systems have been the responsibility of someone acting in a systems librarian role, many times part-time in conjunction with other responsibilities.

In the broadest sense, these systems provide the foundation of automating traditional library services, such as acquisitions and cataloging. In most cases, a library system of this type was the first automation project for a library and remains the singularly most significant component of automation efforts. Responsibilities surrounding these systems include:

1. Planning for and initial implementation of the system.
2. Routine upgrades of hardware and software.
3. Ongoing operational management of the system.
4. Special projects.
5. Planning for and implementation of new modules.
6. Budgeting.
7. Replacement planning.

While some sites may choose to de-emphasize some of these areas of responsibility, all of them must be dealt with in some fashion. It is worth noting that at some libraries a systems librarian will personally perform all of these duties, while at others, he or she may handle some of them directly, delegate and coordinate others, and facilitate the process in yet others. In most cases, this division is a function of site size, complexity, history, and need.

Planning for and initial implementation of the system

Any large project that has as wide-ranging implications as automating entire departments, units, or organizations requires planning and coordination. Systems librarians assist in these processes, many times coordinating project management for the entire implementation. Except in the smallest libraries, this process involves—or should involve—more than just the systems librarian. While many librarians pride themselves on having detailed knowledge about operations in many departments, a project of this magnitude requires input from current staff in all affected areas. There is simply too much to do and very real deadlines in most circumstances (e.g., budgetary constraints for use of funding, contract requirements for completion dates, etc.).

The nature and amount of planning will depend to a large degree on the size of the library, the complexity of the project, and the experience of the staff in implementing technologies of this type. For example, a library that has automated these functions previously and has anticipated a change for some time may have less need for extensive retrospective conversion of printed bibliographic records. It is not unusual, however, for the planning process to consume more than a year, and some components may continue well beyond initial implementation.

A key element in planning is communication, and not just between the systems librarian and others. A systems librarian functioning somewhat as an outsider can facilitate communication among library units in the planning process to ensure that decisions made in one part of the planning process by one unit do not unknowingly preclude options for another unit at a later time.

The actual implementation usually will not go exactly as planned. If it does, great, but experience suggests that the likelihood of that is slim. Effective, structured, and responsible planning, however, can minimize the likelihood that disaster will occur. Implementation includes installation of the hardware, operating system, and application software; database conversion and loading; and establishing initial accounts and security, among other details. Informed systems librarians are crucial at this point. They not only perform many of these tasks, but they also establish important links to the vendor's support staff.

Routine upgrades of hardware and software

No matter how well the planning and implementation processes took place, at some point part of the system will need an upgrade. Such is the nature of computing! Software upgrades are the most common as vendors refine existing modules and add new features. Hardware upgrades are routine as well to accommodate new software, additional databases, or changes in technology. Having someone (e.g., a systems librarian) responsible for tracking these developments and preparing the library for their implementation has become critical as libraries depend more on reliable access to these systems.

Ongoing operational management of the system

Despite what the popular press and science fiction movies might suggest, computers and the software that runs on them are not totally self-sufficient. They require routine management and maintenance. The most complex site to manage is one that employs mainframe technology. In these cases, several specialists may be required to handle operating system maintenance, application software maintenance (the part that libraries actually interact with), communications systems operations, and backup management.

In terms of sheer numbers, most installed library systems are currently running on workstation-level hardware (i.e., Unix hosts) or microcomputers. These systems, perhaps somewhat contrary to popular opinion and marketing literature, also require attention—less attention than mainframes, but attention, nonetheless. For most libraries, the key elements will be operations and performance monitoring and backup management. Vendors whose systems run on workstation-level hardware usually maintain the software themselves (i.e., the library is not responsible for programming). Libraries are responsible for monitoring the system and notifying the vendor when something is not working correctly or something suspicious has occurred.

Special projects

As part of the routine functioning of a library, special projects will always arise. Some of these might be generated by internal needs (e.g., a need to have greater collection information to plan better the acquisition process); others might come from external requests (e.g., users would like to have lists of new items received). These projects require the generation of information from the system. In many cases, the unit needing the information can be empowered to gather and process it on its own. If so, the systems librarian's role would be consultative and instructional. In other cases, there may be an ongoing need to have the systems librarian involved.

Planning for and implementation of new modules

Many libraries purchase the modules of an integrated system separately as they need them or can afford them. In such circumstances, the systems librarian would have the responsibility to lead the ongoing process. In other libraries, all current modules from a vendor may be installed, but new ones are offered from time to time. The systems librarian can ensure that units in the library that would benefit from new modules are aware of what is available, how they work, what trade-offs are implied, and which constraints are entailed. He or she can arrange for a trial or demonstration if that would be helpful.

Budgeting

No matter how much a library's ILS initially costs, ongoing expenditures will occur in the operation of the system. In some cases, a maintenance contract will be purchased on an annual basis for ongoing hardware and software support. In general, additional equipment, such as disk drives, and supplies, such as backup tape cartridges, printer ribbons, and paper, will require line items in a budget.

Replacement planning

After spending thousands, or even millions, of dollars on a new system, one may find it difficult to begin thinking what the next steps might be. Henderson states, "It is a strange quirk of automation that almost at the same time as the technical services librarian plans for a new system, he/she must also plan for obsolescence . . ." (1983, 28). While a system may continue to serve the current needs quite well for many years, there will be new services and features, currently unknown, that a library will need in the future. To be positioned to take advantage of such options in the future, it is important to have people monitoring these developments.

As of this writing, most ILS vendors are marketing or have plans to market versions of their systems that will run on a variety of hardware platforms. This feature is particularly important because it is advantageous to be able to replace the underlying hardware while keeping the same software. This frees a library from being bound to one hardware manufacturer's product line, when for performance or support reasons, a replacement becomes necessary. The reverse is also useful: being able to change software without changing hardware. The wide support for Unix, both for hardware and application software, has provided this flexibility.

Network Design and Management

Nearly every library has or will shortly have some type of network involved in operations. For some, a network connection may simply be a dial-up connection to OCLC, a regional consortium of library catalogs, or the Internet; for others a network may entail thousands of desktop connections, tens of servers and hosts, and backbones that stretch across several buildings or campuses. In either case, and for all of the possibilities in between, someone must be responsible for building and maintaining the network. While it may be desirable for some libraries to outsource this function, doing so does not release the library from the responsibility of participating in and overseeing the process of design, implementation, and management.

As indicated in both of the previously cited surveys (Muir 1995; Muirhead 1994a) and in the growth of network-related literature, the use of and need to be informed about networking technologies has grown tremendously in libraries over the past several years. Systems librarians have commented that this is now a major area of responsibility. Indeed, the development of various networking technologies has significantly impacted the nature of systems librarianship (Lavagnino 1997).

Network design and management can entail a number of component pieces depending to a large degree on the size and complexity of the network. All networking projects are likely to involve some aspects of the following: design and planning, installation and testing, performance monitoring and troubleshooting, ongoing management, and training.

Design and planning

A plethora of books and other resources are available on the market and for free that outline the variety of factors to consider when planning for a network (e.g., Cabral and Ruth 1997; Hancock 1989; Spurgeon 1997; Wittmann 1995). In general, there are technical (e.g., which topology and protocols to employ) and nontechnical (e.g., who gets what kind of access) issues. For some sites, this initial phase could be relatively short. For example, if a library is small and has $5,000 available to invest, there is no point in considering solutions that will cost $10,000 or more. For others who already have networking in place, this could be an ongoing reengineering project that requires coordination with a larger parent organization (e.g., a university or city government).

Network design elements include evaluation of anticipated traffic and use; physical, fiscal, and political constraints; expertise versus functionality trade-offs; performance and growth expectations; and risk factors. Doing it by the book is not always possible, nor productive. For some libraries, the primary goal may be to get as much reliable connectivity as possible organization-wide for $200,000; for others, just getting five computers to share a database for the least possible expense may be the main concern. And still others may be looking toward networking multimedia applications and databases across a metropolitan area. The real goal is to match the level of planning with the size of the project, always keeping in mind that most projects will have future consequences as outgrowths of current decisions.

It is fairly common for vendors of networking products, both manufacturers and resellers, to offer to perform a site visit in which engineers and design technicians survey the physical and logical layout of an organization and make recommendations for purchase. Consultants can also be retained to perform this service. The challenge for libraries is twofold: the library still must make a decision (that cannot be outsourced) and the library must be in a position to evaluate a vendor's or consultant's recommendations. Systems librarians can address this need.

Installation and testing

Once a network design is agreed on and the necessary equipment is purchased, someone must install and test it when it arrives. Networks entail cabling, network hardware (e.g., hubs, routers, servers, etc.), desktop hardware (e.g., network interface cards for each computer), software for each computer, and possibly external network connectivity. Depending on the particular design requirements of the site and the extent of the project, a network installation may also include significant electrical power work; wiring closet construction; cable plant construction; heating, ventilating, and air-conditioning (HVAC) redesign; local telephone company egress arrangements; and furniture design and replacement.

Systems librarians can and do perform and coordinate these activities, but just like the design process, portions of this step can be contracted or outsourced. A library will want to take responsibility for testing to verify that the products meet the goals of the project.

Performance monitoring and troubleshooting

Once a network is installed, it does not run itself. At some point, something will not work as it is supposed to. Someone will need to troubleshoot these problems and resolve them as they occur. Ongoing monitoring can reduce the amount of unexpected failures over the life of the equipment.

Most worthwhile networking equipment can monitor its performance through the network. A standard protocol, Simple Network Management Protocol (SNMP), is used to report statistics and other operational information to a management station on the network.

Some manufacturers charge a little more for their SNMP compatible units, but it is worth every penny on a mission-critical network. Having someone on-site who can perform these valuable functions and understand how the system operates will maintain the value of the initial investment in networking.

Ongoing management

Similar to the previous section, this one deals with the overall management of the network over time, including user adds and changes, equipment repair and replacement, bandwidth utilization monitoring, and growth planning. Having a highly trained staff, armed with powerful management and analytical tools, will ensure the health of a library's network.

Training

Any project as complex as a network requires an investment in training. The systems librarian and staff who support the network will need to be up-to-date on the design, functioning, and management of the particular network installed. Users, particularly staff in the library units using the network, will need to know how to access the network, changes in how their computers operate, what to expect in terms of performance, what resources will be available, and who to call in case of a problem. After investing in all the hardware, software, and construction, it hardly seems wise to ignore the people for whom the network was installed.

Server and Host Administration

Networks usually include servers and hosts that provide access to file space, printing queues, applications, and other resources. These machines can be any type of computer (e.g., ILS, Unix machine, mainframe, etc.) that provides some type of service to its users. As computers become more powerful, more compact, and multifunctional, the distinction between servers and hosts is frequently difficult to make or pointless.

These devices require installation, monitoring and management, and maintenance. Establishing and maintaining user accounts and groups, associating and maintaining rights to services, performance monitoring, backup management, security auditing, and application installation and management are all duties that must be performed on servers and hosts. Common operating systems include: Unix,

VMS, OS/2, Novell NetWare, and Windows NT. A deep knowledge of these environments and the services that can be offered on them (e.g., software applications, file service, Web server hosting, e-mail, print queues, Domain Name Service, routing, network management, etc.) is critical. A training program for users is also necessary for the productive application of these technologies.

Desktop Computing

As serially connected dumb terminals have found their way to obsolete property and garbage heaps, microcomputers have become standard office equipment on staff desktops. These devices now provide a platform of integration that assists staff and the public in accessing a variety of electronic resources and tools. Microcomputers in conjunction with networks create a significant strategic resource for organizations because together they provide a means of enhancing certain types of productivity, increasing access to shared information, and improving the means of communication.

These advantages do come at a cost, however. Microcomputers do not install and maintain themselves, nor do they fix their own problems. Despite what some well-intentioned publications claim about the ability to do computing on the cheap, ultimately an organization that has invested in computing will invest even more money to keep the equipment and services reliable, available, and usable. Some projections on the cost of owning and maintaining microcomputers run as high as $13,000 per year per machine (Gibbs 1997, 87). These estimates are compiled from surveys of businesses. Surveys such as these measure initial purchase and installation, networking, ongoing troubleshooting and maintenance, upgrades, training, and lost productivity because of outages and "futzing" (i.e., goofing around with the computer to get it to do what the user wants).

Part of the cost of providing useful technology is investing in the staff to make it happen. While it is important to understand that libraries will probably never spend the amount of money that some businesses do on information technology, any planning that does not take into consideration the total cost of ownership is shortsighted. (See Chapter 5, "Technical Management," "Purchasing and Total Cost Analysis.")

Training, Documentation, and Support

It is ironic that an organization can spend thousands of dollars on technology and not a dime on the materials required to use it effectively, but this does happen. In libraries, one of the most common areas of responsibility for systems librarians is training, documentation, and support. People in these positions are actively involved in providing one-on-one assistance and group sessions both formally and informally on the use of ILS applications, word processing and spreadsheets, database searching, e-mail, Web searching, HTML, and many more. Creating a written record of how things work and what steps to do to resolve particular problems is critical to a well-functioning systems department and library technology program.

Support can entail a number of different facets; this section focuses on general technology support that could include software (e.g., How do I paste this entry into this window?), hardware (e.g., The command key on my keyboard doesn't work.), or requisition consultation (e.g., What programs will help me streamline my workflow?). The more direct support that is available to staff, the higher the return on investment in technology.

Application Development

Some libraries develop software in-house. Historically, the major software development project in a library has been the ILS, but with the growth in commercial ILS products in the past two decades, the focus has changed to other important, but smaller, endeavors. Applications run the gamut from local information databases to specialized software, to utilities that run in the background, to multimedia presentations, to Web cgi Perl scripts and Java applets. It is not uncommon for much of this development to take place throughout library units, not just in the systems office. With the availability of tools to assist in programming in high-level computer languages, development can be easily distributed as needed. Systems librarians not only develop applications, but they also train staff to become self-sufficient in these areas.

Planning and Budget

Clarke (1982, 36) wrote: "Any sufficiently advanced technology is indistinguishable from magic." To harness the magic without shattering the budget, libraries must plan. To avoid being bitten by the magic without losing sight of the plan, libraries must budget. Technology plans can consume an enormous amount of energy—some of it needless. Nonetheless, having a direction with identifiable, measurable goals is useful to keep a library on track. Without some planning a library could end up with one unit having more computing power than it can consume, while another is so outdated that increases in productivity are impossible and staff morale is abysmal. Or every new computing fad is pursued, while ongoing core applications suffer.

Systems librarians can and do provide assistance in constructing a technology agenda in consultation with others in the library. Any worthwhile plan must include some source of funding to make it happen, but not all plans can be funded. Wise stewardship of resources demands a set of priorities that can be met as funds become available. Being able to say "yes" and "no" are equally important in all plans and budgets.

Specification and Purchasing

One of the growing areas of importance in systems work is the creation of adequate, accurate, and incontrovertible technical specifications. As computing becomes more popular, the common perception is that all computers and computing devices are commodity items, meaning that the only difference between one manufacturer and another is the price. While this is becoming true for several components of computing (e.g., hard disk drives, mice, and CD-ROM drives), it remains uncertain for others (e.g., motherboards, memory, monitors, power supplies, and keyboards). The old adage of getting what one pays for holds true in many cases with computers and computing devices.

The reason for enforcing rigorous specifications is not to spend more than one must to acquire a useful and appropriate device—indeed writing specifications and adhering to them costs time and money. Rather, the point is to ensure that one receives what one expects and that the reliability and performance of the item are adequate.

The context of a particular purchase will guide the level of detail that is necessary. For example, if a library needs three local printers, a few moments invested can determine the requirement for impact versus ink jet, quality of print desired, and speed. Spending hours poring over detailed specifications for a printer that costs

$150 is not a wise investment of time. On the other hand, if a library needs a server that will support 300 simultaneous log-ins, integrate into an existing protocol environment, and run a current set of applications, then significant investments of time in verifying compliance and overall performance can make the difference between a satisfactory and unsatisfactory result. Thus, technical specifications are extremely important to ensure that the library receives the quality of product that was intended.

Furthermore, libraries affiliated with public institutions are particularly bound by purchasing restrictions and open bid processes—all the more reason to construct watertight specifications. (See Chapter 5, "Technical Management," "Purchasing and Total Cost Analysis.") The creative work of a diligent systems librarian on a single purchase can pay for his or her salary and benefits for that year.

Another aspect of specification and purchasing is standards. Adhering to industry and local standards can reduce performance and compatibility problems in the future. Increasingly, libraries require the flexibility to replace hardware or software without replacing an entire system or series of systems. Often proprietary solutions lock an organization into one vendor's vision or set of solutions. Standards assist in avoiding this trap.

Standards, however, are not a guarantee of near-perfect solutions. Many times a standards-compliant solution may not perform at the same level as a proprietary one that is designed to address one particular problem directly. While standards are created to ensure that one part of a vendor's system can talk to another part of another vendor's system, every computing environment, even those designed with standards in mind, will include proprietary components. Determining the need for, alternatives to, and implications of standards-based technical solutions is prime intellectual territory for systems librarians.

Local purchasing standards are important as well. Many organizations decide to acquire and support certain hardware configurations or software packages. These decisions—local standards—permit technical staff to focus energy on installing, maintaining, and supporting a manageable universe of technology. While some local standards—or the fact that they exist at all—are controversial for some users, they are necessary to deploy wisely an organization's resources. Unfortunately, some users believe that they should be able to do whatever they wish with an organization's technology. And some users naively believe that all technology is at a stage in which any hardware and software will seamlessly interoperate. These sets of beliefs create an environment in which technical staff acting on these standards are forced into a philosophical argument that cannot be resolved. One way around the issue is for systems librarians to involve others in the organization in these decisions and to inform users why such standards exist and how they assist in the efficient investment and deployment of technology within the organization.

Technology Exploration and Evaluation

One of the most challenging and exciting areas of systems librarianship is the involvement with emerging technologies. This component of the job is similar to research and development. Many technologies that are developed for other industries have applications within libraries and information environments. In conjunction with colleagues from around the library, a systems librarian has the opportunity to track new developments or to find new applications of technology already on the market.

Product evaluation is a significant part of systems librarianship. While vendor representatives may suggest strongly that a new product is exactly what the library needs to address a certain problem, it would be naive for any librarian to assume that such a solution will work without further investigation. In many cases it is appropriate to request a trial of the product before the decision to pursue it is made. These tests may be as straightforward as arranging for a thirty-day trial of a new version of software or as complex as setting up a separate network for testing a remote access solution.

The implications of advanced technology are an area of growing concern within libraries and society as a whole. Understanding the trade-offs of implementing one type of technology over another or in the level of technology investment is critical for all librarians. Those in systems work have a responsibility to see that others in the profession are aware of the implications and that appropriate policy and practice issues are addressed.

Miscellaneous Technology Support

Each organization has items that do not fit into neat categories or peculiar responsibilities that get assigned to individuals within the organization based on less-than-obvious logic. Systems librarians have been known to be responsible for telephone systems, satellite technology, emergency alarm systems, teleconferencing studios, classroom support, audiovisual equipment, and a host of other areas or technologies that require a keen sensitivity to detail, technical prowess, sheer tenacity, and a willingness to learn.

Technical Risk Management

Organizations of all sizes must be aware of the risks involved in deploying technology. These risks range from hardware and software failure to privacy invasion, emergency weather damage, and security breaches. Increasingly, libraries have a need to invest in planning and policy making related to technical risks. Systems librarians are key individuals within organizations to lead the effort. They bring to the table a broad understanding of the technology and technical issues as well as the library and human issues. One of the largest areas to address is training users throughout the library to be aware of what is at risk and what is really happening in the use of various technologies. Many risks can be minimized with a modicum of effort.

Communication and Coordination

To paraphrase a comment from many real-estate agents: "There are three things that determine the value of a systems librarian: communication, communication, and communication." The sections outlined previously deal mainly with technical issues that are important and should not be dismissed. In addition to excellent technical skill and knowledge, a systems librarian must possess extraordinary human communication skills. Contrary to one widely held myth, systems units are not a location to which one should migrate noncommunicative staff members.

On the surface, it is obvious that someone who will be involved in training will need to have reasonable skills in this area. These skills apply, however, in other areas as well. Systems librarians are called on to translate highly technical processes and procedures into language that laypeople can understand and benefit from, and they are required to inform other technical people about the needs of libraries and their users in technical language and logic that makes sense to them. In addition, many times systems librarians will need to communicate with vendors that do not serve the library community directly or to agencies and individuals outside the routine library world. Thus, the single most important fundamental skill of a successful systems librarian is communication. This skill will smooth system migration; improve service and expectations for service; lead to effective negotiations with vendors, other information technology units within the organization, other library departments, city governments, etc.; increase the likelihood of getting what is needed; and facilitate greater ownership of the whole "system."

In contrast, however, the emphasis of strong communication skills should not imply any lack of technical facility. Both sets of skills are needed to succeed. In fact, both sets can work synergistically. For example, a systems librarian who can clearly explain a technical detail to a library colleague must possess the technical knowledge in the first place to accomplish the task. The process of communicating in such a fashion builds confidence in the abilities of the systems librarian in carrying out responsibilities on behalf of the library, its staff, and its users.

Many, if not most, systems librarians are involved in coordinating activities with other units within the library or outside the library. In some cases these duties might be formal liaison work with a computing center or data processing unit; in others they might be overseeing contractual relationships with vendors. From the drafting of agreements to the delivery, or nondelivery, of service, it is critical to have someone representing the library who can not only understand and communicate the nature of the library's needs, but also negotiate reasonable alternatives when life becomes less than perfect.

Computing is one of those areas in life in which expectations frequently surpass the ability of the technology to deliver. In part this situation exists because of the marketing hype that inundates the world, but a user's personal experience plays a large role in establishing expectations, too—both high and low ones. Systems librarians in their communication with others in their respective organizations participate in creating levels of expectation. They can assist users ahead of time in knowing what is reasonable to expect. This area might be called "surprise management." While serendipitous surprises can generate creativity at times, they are frequently seen as unwanted hurdles on the path to accomplishing goals.

A special area within communication and coordination is vendor relations. Libraries commonly deal with tens, if not hundreds, of vendors for goods and services of various types. Systems librarians may deal with as many just for technology. Some may be for database products, others may be for networking equipment, and still others may be for desktop computers and peripherals. Maintaining productive relationships with these suppliers and coordinating the resolution of difficulties among several of them is a primary responsibility of many systems librarians.

Much of the work of systems librarians entails communicating with and among members of their two professions. In many ways, systems librarians provide a translation service between these respective professions. Again, strong communication skills are an absolute necessity.

From this discussion of common responsibilities for systems librarians, it is clear that the individuals in these positions cover a diversity of areas. They are required to have breadth and depth in their knowledge and skill. In addition, many librarians performing systems duties also contribute to other areas within their respective libraries (e.g., cataloging, reference, circulation, etc.).

Specific Skill Sets

So, what are the specific skill sets that facilitate quality library systems management? The following list of skill categories has been gleaned from recent job descriptions for systems-related positions, a review of the literature, and my experience and observations. The categories are a further refinement of the responsibilities previously covered and reflect the diversity of skills required for these positions. Within the categories specific items are further explicated. This list is not exhaustive, but is rather a beginning foundation on which additional skills will be built over time.

Library skills

Data structures related to library materials

Familiarity and experience using data structures common in libraries and other information environments, knowledge of current metadata initiatives.

MARC records

Knowledge of the record structure and use in libraries, ability to use management software to manipulate the record and load records into multiple systems, understanding of the value of structured records and standards and the relationship of MARC to recent related Internet standards and conventions.

Library services and administrative structures

Familiarity with typical library organizational structures and the services, responsibilities, and needs associated with each unit.

Mission

Knowledge of the mission of libraries in general and any related local variances.

Research process

Conceptual understanding of the research process, familiarity with statistical analysis, experience gained from graduate course work.

Knowledge organization and classification

Deep understanding of schema used in organizing and retrieving knowledge, awareness of classification trade-offs, familiarity with common library data structures.

Information retrieval

Familiarity with variety of access and retrieval methodologies and technologies, experience with multiple database designs, conceptual understanding of trade-offs among design and products used in retrieving information.

Information policy

Awareness of local, regional, and national issues and initiatives related to information policy; understanding of societal and technical implications of policy positions; commitment to service in light of a diversity of concerns.

Library automation skills

Automated functions

Basic familiarity with the typical library functions that are automated (e.g., circulation, acquisitions, serials, cataloging, online catalogs, reference databases, interlibrary loan, etc.) and knowledge of data, management, and service interdependencies among these integrated components.

Vendors

> Awareness of companies offering solutions to automate these traditional functions and their respective histories.

Products

> Knowledge of available product lines and experience in using one or more components of one or more vendors.

Requests for information (RFIs)/requests for proposals (RFPs)

> Understanding of specification creation, need for details, and testing and verification processes.

Contracts

> Basic knowledge of the nature of contracts.

Hardware/software

> Conceptual knowledge of system components and operations, demonstrated ability to translate documentation into operations, sufficient process knowledge to articulate areas of responsibility, and hands-on use of multiuser systems.

Computing

Desktop operating systems

> Conceptual knowledge of the function of desktop operating systems, significant use of more than one of the following: Macintosh OS; Windows 3.1, 95, and NT; OS/2; or Unix.

Server, midrange, and mainframe operating systems

> Conceptual knowledge of the function of host, server, and network operating systems; significant use of more than one of the following: Unix; VMS; MVS or VM/CMS; NetWare; or Windows NT Server.

Programming

> Exposure to structured, modular programming; experience constructing a utility that performs read, write, display, data manipulation, and flow-control functions; familiarity with one or more of the following: Assembly,

BASIC, C, Cobol, Pascal, or Perl; exposure to object-oriented environments such as C++ or Java.

Database design

Conceptual understanding of design elements and implications, experience designing and programming a database for input and retrieval using variant data types (e.g., text and images) in at least three different environments, one of which operates on a multiuser platform.

Troubleshooting

Familiarity with mechanisms for identifying, tracking, isolating, and resolving common computing problems; experience working in a support environment.

System design

Familiarity with common design elements and challenges (both theoretical and practical), exposure to human factors research, experience working with a design team.

Networking

Network design

Conceptual understanding of network architectures, design parameters, modeling, and implications; knowledge of current and near-future technologies.

Network services

Knowledge of file and print services available in a variety of LAN environments, knowledge of other services available in typical local and wide area networks (e.g., name resolution, time synchronization, routing, etc.), experience installing and managing such services.

Protocols

Familiarity with common network protocols (e.g., TCP/IP, IPX/SPX, AppleTalk, OSI, etc.); experience installing, configuring, and using a protocol on at least one platform.

Network applications

> Knowledge of issues surrounding network-based applications, including technical, legal, financial, and security aspects; conceptual understanding of relevant design principles for network applications; experience installing and configuring a network application.

Network management

> Familiarity with network management principles, awareness of options and implications for managing objects on a network, exposure to network management protocols (e.g., SNMP) and applications.

Internet technologies

> Familiarity with current technologies employed in the Internet, including, but not limited to, routing, Web-related programming and design, interactive systems, and database integration; ability to translate data/knowledge structures into meaningful retrieval environments; conceptual understanding of all components involved in information delivery over the Internet.

Management

Basic management

> Familiarity with management principles, schools of thought, and sources of additional information; exposure to accounting, auditing, purchasing, and quality control practices.

Technical management

> Familiarity with the application of management principles to technical units, awareness of variances from other work environments, work experience in a technical unit.

Resource management

> Conceptual understanding of principles related to matching resources and needs, ability to focus on identified organizational priorities.

Security and risk management

Basic familiarity with problem sets, conceptual knowledge of available solutions, ability to balance competing requirements.

General

Ethics

Familiarity with ethics literature in general and that related to information technology, exposure to the ethical challenges inherent in the deployment and use of information technology, participation in analysis of case studies relating to ethics.

Communication

Demonstrated human interaction skills, familiarity with conflict resolution and stress-management techniques.

Training

Experience instructing users, familiarity with instructional design and technology.

It is likely to be difficult to find a person who excels in all these cognitive and behavioral areas, but systems work at a minimum entails these issues and skills. Certainly, local variations exist to the degree that some systems librarians may focus primarily on pragmatic issues related solely to an integrated library system, while others function mainly as liaisons with computing people. Be that as it may, across the profession, systems librarians—and those who are called something else, but are performing systems functions—on the whole are called on to be involved in these areas in significant ways.

Roles for Systems Librarians

Another approach to defining systems librarianship is to examine the roles that these people play in their respective organizations, as opposed to looking only at common sets of responsibilities. A role describes more of the influence and function of a person or position rather than the specific duties.

Designer

Many systems librarians provide a great deal of input into the design of software for large and small applications. Some library vendors even seek out this input. Certainly others in libraries who use various systems should have input as well. The perspective that systems librarians bring to the table, however, combines a knowledge of library operations, organizational data flow, hardware and operating system implications, data structures, interface design principles, computer and network performance characteristics, and organizational resources.

Planner

Planning takes on a variety of forms in libraries. Some systems librarians are involved in planning and budget issues for the library as a whole, functioning as senior administrators within the organization. Others are involved in project planning in a consultative role with other units and departments assisting them in determining the most appropriate direction to take, and in identifying areas in which automation or systems support is appropriate.

Implementor

By far one of the most significant and common roles systems librarians play is implementor. From small-scale projects, such as identifying and evaluating software for scheduling, to large mainframe installations, systems librarians can be found right in the middle of this activity.

Consultant

Systems librarians have a perspective to contribute to many of the projects that are undertaken in a library. Many projects that are not on the whole technology-based do, in fact, have technology components or implications. For example, building renovations frequently require technology assessments and design factors. Changes in electrical circuits or HVAC equipment may have implications for computing, or computing may have an impact on basic building mechanical systems. Systems librarians can also provide consultative support regarding emerging technologies that might have application in the library for the future. Any feasibility study or analysis should include a systems librarian.

Technology Representative

Both within and outside of the library, systems librarians are technology representatives—offering information regarding the technologies themselves and the library's plans for them. Most libraries have parent organizations of some type; frequently these organizations have formal or informal technology committees or groups on which systems librarians serve, representing the interests of libraries. There are also consortial, regional, and national technology organizations in which systems librarians participate as representatives.

Facilitator

Systems librarians encourage the use and development of technologies where they are appropriate and can benefit libraries and their users. Systems librarians also can work to get projects and people back on track in cases in which something has gone awry. Facilitators such as these are able to encourage people to think systematically about solutions to problems by demonstrating the behavior themselves. Working together on projects with departments and units throughout the organization, systems librarians may be uniquely positioned to assist them in dealing with overlapping issues and interdependent contingencies.

Once again, it is clear that systems librarians carry a full plate of responsibilities and roles with their respective organizations.

Qualities, Approaches, and Attitudes

The discussion thus far has focused on the variety of things that systems librarians may do as a part of their jobs. In surveying the nature of systems librarianship, it is just as important to devote some time to the qualities, approaches, and attitudes that are advantageous for a systems librarian to possess regardless of his or her professional background.

Flexibility and Balance

Because of the breadth and depth of the responsibilities of systems librarians, two fundamental qualities for people in these positions are flexibility and balance. In carrying out their duties, systems librarians must be able to move from issue to issue and project to project with equal aplomb, sometimes at a moment's notice. At the same time, they need to keep in mind the relative priority of the duties at hand and a sense of the interdependence among projects. To keep things on track and avoid details falling between the cracks, they also must see outside of the current project, even while in it.

Sound Judgment

Because of the sensitive nature of many of the issues with which systems librarians deal, sound judgment is required. From negotiating project timelines and resolving computing problems in an effective fashion to mediating personnel issues, systems librarians must employ competent judgment. This trait develops over time as a person is exposed to a variety of challenges and is able to work through them. Personnel with highly developed senses of judgment gained through years of experience in an organization offer significant value to libraries. This trait should not be taken lightly.

Curiosity and Risk Taking

Because systems work frequently involves dancing with the unknown, curiosity and risk taking are important qualities for a systems librarian. While these two qualities may be difficult to measure and can create challenges when found in large doses, they are valuable nonetheless. Curiosity draws an individual into exploring something at hand (e.g., Why won't this application print? Why does this workstation not see the server on the network? Or, how can the library fund a network expansion?). Risk taking provides the daring to challenge the status quo and develop something new (e.g., a new solution, a new perspective, or a new organization). These two in combination drive successful experimentation.

Follow-Through and Persistence

If curiosity and risk taking begin the process, follow-through and persistence complete the package. In pure scientific research, the experimenter is not driven to find a conclusion that generates immediate results for new products or services; libraries operate on a different plane, however. Therefore, while exploration is absolutely necessary, the goal is to fix something or to create new or better products and services. That being the case, systems librarians must persist to achieve these goals. Whether it involves troubleshooting a difficult computer problem, designing a new public interface, or forcing a vendor to comply with a contract, "it ain't over till it's over."

Time Management

Part of the process of successfully resolving challenges, whether technical or otherwise, is having a sense of relative importance about the current issues at hand and a willingness to devote an appropriate amount of time to these problems, given existing constraints. Time management has become a popular topic in business not just because it is trendy, but also because it is necessary as responsibilities grow. In a nutshell, time management entails acknowledging time as a limited resource, determining the items that demand one's attention, prioritizing those that do, and accepting that some things will not receive one's attention. Given the demands placed on a systems librarian's time, such skills and mental attitudes are essential.

Resource Management

A resource management perspective likewise is essential. It is important to see people, time, processes, equipment, and data, among other things, as resources with value and limitations. Systems librarians should act with sound judgment in weighing and applying these resources in combination toward achieving organizational goals. An attitude of preserving, cultivating, and replenishing all resources is critical—in a word, stewardship. (See Chapter 5, "Technical Management," "Resource Management.")

Firmness and Cooperativeness

Balance was previously mentioned as a key element. Systems librarians must balance firmness and cooperativeness as they perform their duties in an organization. Nothing great can be accomplished on one's own; cooperation provides the fuel for achieving organizational goals. At the same time, firmness establishes boundaries to protect organizational and personal values. Neither of these attitudes will work effectively by itself, each must be present in equal measure.

Nonjudgmental Approach

Along with firmness and cooperation comes a nonjudgmental approach. To function effectively in multiple arenas as an advocate for librarians and libraries, vendors, and other technical people, systems librarians must recognize and communicate that none of the players is always right or always wrong. Whenever possible, a focus on moving forward toward a shared goal (e.g., getting the job done) will produce a better outcome. For example, continuing to argue with a vendor about a contract item when clear definitional differences between the library's understanding and the vendor's understanding exist is nonproductive. Redefining the terms, if possible, removes a barrier and provides an opportunity to find a resolution. Similarly, discussions among library departments frequently can suffer from a lack of shared meanings. Claiming that one meaning is correct and all others are incorrect will not speed closure. In cases such as this, no progress can be made until that initial difference is addressed on some level. Encouraging such an attitude also frees individuals to admit when they are wrong in some fashion and to move on with life.

Skepticism

Effective systems work requires an approach that is questioning, critical, and skeptical in nature. Sometimes an approach of this type earns the holder a moniker of negativity. Be that as it may, systems librarians to resolve technical problems, to plan adequate implementations, and to maintain existing services must question all information provided by any source. In computing, both from the industry and from users, misinformation runs rampant. The only known cure is to adopt a skeptical attitude toward this information. This approach, however, is not a license to be curmudgeonly or nasty; it is an insurance policy for realism.

Technical Realism

Technical realism is also a becoming attribute for systems librarians. This quality balances a love of "cool" technology with an awareness of organizational needs and goals. It also entails understanding and communicating the difference between possibility (i.e., Can it be done?) and feasibility (i.e., Is it appropriate for this library?).

Analytical, Methodical Serendipity

The resolution of many problems demands a methodology that documents stepwise progress through a series of logical stages. This method is akin to flow controls in programming in which a series of conditions can be tested, such as if this, then that, else something different, or while this is true, do that. Approaching problem resolution in this fashion through asking questions and testing outcomes is often very effective. Any experienced troubleshooter, however, will explain that many answers, or more general approaches to resolution, are discovered through serendipitous elements in the process. One could argue that logical analysis and serendipity are at odds with one another; such is not necessarily the case. The two avenues work quite nicely together and provide a strong set of tools for resolving problems.

Perspective Switching

Switching perspectives on a dime—the forest-and-trees scenario—is a greatly needed ability for systems librarians. Some days are filled with detail-oriented projects such as troubleshooting an application that is not performing as stated or determining why two devices refuse to talk to each other. Other days are crammed with planning meetings and presentations to constituents. And then there are the days that bounce back and forth in a rather schizophrenic manner: one minute attention is needed to debug a program, the next requires personnel management finesse, followed by a network segment failure. The aptitude for and comfort with these wide swings in focus is essential for people in systems positions. The details and the large picture are equally important simultaneously.

Fire in the Belly

Like other professionals, systems librarians are driven by a desire to accomplish something: make more information resources conveniently available to patrons, integrate disparate databases into a uniform delivery mechanism, extend a network throughout an organization, automate processing-oriented tasks, create an interactive Web presence, etc. No matter what the end goal is, the drive, or fire in the belly, must be present. This quality may manifest itself in many ways: dedication to organizational goals; leadership in new projects; involvement in local, regional, or national organizations that support similar goals; going beyond minimum expectations; working cooperatively with others in an organization; experimenting with different ways of accomplishing tasks; or investing in personal professional development and technical expertise, to list a few.

Resiliency

Just like the equipment they manage, systems librarians must be fault-tolerant and resilient. With the demands of the job bearing down on them and with all these qualities, approaches, and attitudes expected in addition, it would be reasonable to shut down occasionally. Systems librarianship is not for the faint of heart; it is a fast-paced, demanding specialty. But it is doable! The people who choose this avenue should be able to roll with the punches and come back after a fall. While the notion of thick skin usually implies cold indifference to others, there is another sense for this notion: not wearing one's feelings on one's sleeve. In this case it could be an effective success strategy for systems librarians.

Technical Aptitude

Systems librarianship is a mix of technical and nontechnical elements. As important as the nontechnical portions are for effective service in this profession, they should not overshadow the need for technical aptitude. Systems librarianship is a technical field that focuses on computing and networking in a library context. Even if a particular library does not call on its systems librarian to perform hands-on information technology management, the data from the field indicate that a solid technical understanding of these issues is needed. Systems librarians, therefore, are "techies." This can be learned, just as librarianship is learned. The best systems librarians combine expertise in both professional areas in fashions that serve their organizations and constituencies.

Systems Positions: Librarian or Computer Specialist?

Having presented the responsibilities, roles, and attributes of systems librarians, one should spend some time discussing what professional background is most appropriate for such positions. The decision to hire either a librarian or a computer specialist for systems work is hotly debated (Boyce and Heim 1988; Martin 1988; McLain, Wallace, and Heim 1990; Oberg and Kelm 1997; White 1991). Most of these discussions ignore the fact that in reality both backgrounds are successfully represented in the field, and a number of people have both professional backgrounds.

The literature that attempts to address part of this issue tends to focus on which sets of skills can be more easily acquired on the job. Thus, the question is posed: is it more effective to train a librarian in computing technology or to train a computer specialist in library operations? This question and the answers given to it are essential for employers to discuss; the asking of it reflects a realism in libraries. Libraries do not have endless financial resources to apply to systems work—or any other work for that matter. A decision to hire a systems person frequently means not creating another position elsewhere in the organization or reassigning an existing position line. The number of systems librarians indicating that they have responsibilities in other areas of their libraries suggests the additive nature of these positions (i.e., they have been crafted out of a mixture of other positions).

It would be important, therefore, to consider what background is most beneficial to a library. To get at this issue, however, requires an honest, nonconfrontational review of competencies in both professions and their respective preparatory preservice educational programs. Accomplishing such a task is extremely difficult for a variety of reasons: lack of universal standards on professional competencies in both areas, wide variances in preservice curricula, and nonacademic characteristics that elude examination, to name a few. Perhaps the greatest obstacle to such a review, however, is that the person conducting it is likely to have been indoctrinated into one or the other of these professions and simultaneously totally naive toward the other. It is also helpful to understand from the beginning of such a review that the outcome is likely to be somewhat ambiguous, or less than convincing, for libraries that have successfully employed systems people with different backgrounds from the ones listed in a recommendation.

These challenges having been noted, perhaps it is best to focus instead on what is represented in the field and to identify characteristics that are necessary in the candidates being considered for systems positions (such as those identified previously) regardless of professional background. Not all computer people are devoid of understanding libraries, just as not all librarians are devoid of understanding computers. Such an approach might assist in defusing the intense debate on this issue.

Perhaps the intensity of this debate has been heightened because of the approaches that view the outcome as potentially damaging to librarianship. It is not necessary, however, to see things in only this way. If the decision to select a librarian for such a post is based solely on a belief that technical knowledge and skill are simpler to acquire than library science knowledge and skill, the debate will stall on professional turf and not proceed. Likewise, if the decision to select a computer specialist is based solely on a belief that library science knowledge and skill are simpler to acquire than computer science or MIS knowledge and skill, the question still remains unanswered in any generalizable fashion. The point here is that the nature of the debate must change for libraries to move forward on the issue and manage the effective application of information technology without undue energy being focused on who's in what position. It is more productive to focus on fostering the multiple sets of necessary competencies than it is to continue to argue on professional turf issues.

Libraries need to employ people who have strong backgrounds in both library operations and heavy-duty computing and networking technologies. Given this need, libraries face significant challenges in finding appropriately prepared professionals to hire. In addition to hiring well-trained and informed technical professionals with a willingness to "get the job done," libraries must continue to ensure that all staff are informed about technology, both its use and its implications. Focusing solely on either policy issues or technological advancement will not serve libraries well. Balance is key. For if the people in the organization are knowledgeable about policy issues, but do not possess operational skill, they are ignorant of the technological possibilities. On the other hand, if they have acquired significant skill in using technologies, but lack understanding of policy issues, they will be driven by "the next best thing" syndrome and risk falling prey to technological determinism.

The Making of a Systems Librarian

The responsibilities, roles, and contributions of systems librarians are truly diverse and significant. Many of these specific areas are not the sole province of systems librarianship. Indeed, some of the identified topics are prime candidates for shared responsibility and partnerships with other librarians. A systems librarian can offer a unique perspective, however, to many of the special projects and operational challenges within libraries.

The knowledge, duties, and attitudes discussed here constitute a foundation of systems librarianship. These attributes in part are shared with other librarians and with computer specialists that may come from computer science, MIS, or engineering backgrounds. This specialty within librarianship represents a unique blend of the ideals to which both professional families aspire.

3

The Education of a Systems Librarian

You grieve you learn
You choke you learn
You laugh you learn
You choose you learn
You pray you learn
You ask you learn
You live you learn

—Alanis Morissette,
You Learn

Perhaps the people working outside of a technical field get the impression that technical professionals are born knowing what they know—a sixth sense so to speak; such is not the case. The preparation and ongoing professional development of systems librarians represent a significant challenge to library education. A variety of concerns about general library education exists, many of them voiced repeatedly in the literature. Library schools have adjusted curricula, changed school names, hired faculty with nonlibrary backgrounds, merged with other departments, and established stronger ties with their respective universities—all with the goal of improving the pre-service education of librarians (or information professionals) and heightening the awareness of the significant role that this profession can play in an information society. To a large degree, these activities have succeeded in changing the orientation of library schools and have provided exposure to different coursework for the students enrolled there (Dalrymple 1997; Marcum 1997; Ostler and Dahlin 1995).

The focus, however, has generally been across-the-board education of librarians, with the hope of preparing professionals who have the background and conceptual understanding to deal with information in all its forms and the tools and technologies necessary to manage its acquisition, maintenance, and use. These are laudable goals and accomplishments, even if they are not particularly new. The actual content of such changes has varied from school to school depending to some extent on the influence of faculty, current students, alumni, other schools, employers, business models, economic forces, higher education reform, etc. The literature has emphasized a variety of areas requiring attention: information management; information science; operations research; systems analysis; system design; system installation and management; programming; access and organization of information; database design; bibliographic control systems; information-retrieval systems; technology evaluation; advanced computing; research methods; statistics; public policy; management; flexibility and innovation; and practica in library automation, to list a few (Boyce and Heim 1988; Corbin 1988; Fisher 1994; McLain, Wallace, and Heim 1990).

These additions and changes to the average curriculum are indeed useful for all library students to experience as a part of basic education for the profession, although many of the topics are again not particularly new. What of education for systems librarians? Certainly these areas of study are appropriate for the student wishing to specialize in systems work, but more is needed. Some schools offer opportunities for students to study "hot topics" such as Web design, Internet retrieval, or multimedia development. These studies, while important and appropriate to cover, are really the purview of all librarians, not just the ones focusing on systems work. There appears to be significant confusion over what every librarian should understand about technology and the specialization and in-depth training needed for those who wish to devote their careers to this role within the profession.

Challenges to Library Schools

Boyce and Heim have outlined a number of the concerns and challenges that library schools and the profession as a whole face regarding the recruitment and training of systems people. Library school entrants tend not to be prepared in math, science, or computing; it is difficult to offer graduate credit for what is perceived as undergraduate content or remedial work; students with computer backgrounds can earn higher salaries even without the additional degree; and it is difficult to convince a student who is immediately hireable with an undergraduate degree to pursue graduate work (Boyce and Heim 1988, 73–74).

With regard to the challenge of providing basic computer literacy for graduate credit, library schools are not alone. Students in many graduate programs, particularly those of interest to nontraditional students (i.e., somewhat older, returning students), have a great need to be brought up-to-date on the use of computing as it relates to the discipline being studied.

Introductory computing classes can be found in communications, education, history, literature, management, music, psychology, social work, etc. This phenomenon is to be expected in a situation in which basic skills in all professions are being redefined and students are returning to school to retool. Library schools are not alone.

Frequently, the literature on librarianship notes the tendency for students in library schools to come from Humanities and Social Science backgrounds. Experience suggests that hiring a science reference librarian, cataloger, or collection development officer can be a challenge if a science background is a prerequisite. In the small body of literature on systems librarianship, the fact that most librarians lack a scientific or technical background is cited as well as a potential detriment to their qualifications for systems positions.

On the surface this comment appears reasonable and consistent with expectations. On a deeper level, however, it carries a dangerous set of assumptions that can thwart the contributions that many systems librarians make to the profession and to the clientele they serve. One would be foolish to argue that there is no value, or less value, in employing a technically savvy librarian in such a position, but to grasp the impact of these assumptions, one must understand what a systems librarian does as previously outlined, what skills and approaches are effective in carrying out those responsibilities, what knowledge and skill can be acquired from Humanities and Social Science training as well as scientific and technical training, what variance is likely to occur among training programs or schools, what assumptions are frequently made about each of these disciplines, and how one's worldview of scientific and technical things or ideas shapes the approach one takes toward people working in technical positions.

What a Systems Librarian Does

Previously, the nature of systems work has been addressed, but an example of the type of work conducted by systems librarians will serve as an illustration for this section. It is common for systems librarians to be responsible for administering an integrated library system that might include creating and modifying accounts, troubleshooting modules that do not operate as indicated, modifying the system to accommodate requests from users of the system, and negotiating support from the vendor.

What Skills Are Required?

These responsibilities require not only a well-rounded understanding of what the system is supposed to do and how it is supposed to work—a primarily, but not entirely, technical issue, but also a solid understanding of the organization served, an approach that accommodates ambiguity, a willingness to perform and experience with highly detail-oriented work, command of several vocabularies and communication styles, and the ability to plan and execute change.

Where Can These Skills Be Learned?

While these skills may be learned in technical and scientific curricula, they are also presented in the humanities and social science disciplines, perhaps more than many people recognize. For example, an anthropologist learns to analyze details and relationships collected in ethnographies similar to a computer scientist examining and debugging programming code. Historians learn to investigate local, regional, and global influences on events and the complex interrelationships among people and their activities—a skill that easily transfers to understanding an organization and its component parts. Musicians struggle to perfect a performance through repeated practice and execution and deal with variances in interpretation of minute details—skills that apply to the perseverence necessary to follow up on ambiguous technical problems until they are resolved.

Large research projects, particularly group projects, teach students how to plan and implement and to work within a schedule, accepting trade-offs as they go. These assignments occur across the curriculum with no one discipline having a corner on such teaching methods.

The point is that many of the useful skills, knowledge, and experience that create an effective systems librarian can be gained from a variety of backgrounds—and none of the possibilities is less valid. It is also worth noting that one computer science program is not the same as another, just like one history program is not the same as another. That is to say that any attempt to codify exactly what initial prerequisites should be for systems librarians will fail to the degree that it is based on an assumption of uniformity of formal training. Guidelines are helpful, but vamping is more realistic!

One caveat to note is that some readers will jump to the conclusion that the skills discussed here can be gained from a variety of sources precisely because they are not technical. This conclusion, while expected, is unfortunate because it reveals a misunderstanding of technical work and training. These skills are, in fact, the heart of technical work. Yes, programming and circuit design are also part of some technical work, but these additional components do not preclude systems analysis, project management, design, and user testing—all of which are portions of many technical degrees and certainly fill the time of systems librarians.

The one entity not mentioned thus far is the amount of math required in a technical program. While this component may represent a significant variance, one must recognize that math plays a large role in the research conducted in many other disciplines as well.

Assumptions and Worldview Influences

Many assumptions about science and technology are prevalent in the general population. Some of these even influence the highly educated. Some common ones are:

> Science and technology are rigid and singular for they do
> not change over time and there are specific solutions to
> problems if one can only find them.
>
> Science and technology are not ambiguous; the only
> ambiguity comes from the poor practice of science.
>
> In science and technology only the details matter; there is
> no interest in broader issues.
>
> The outcomes of science and technology can be controlled.

Nelkin (1995) reviews how notions such as these are promulgated in the press and general science reporting. The degree to which these statements are accepted will influence the believer's view of people working in scientific and technical careers and of the preparation necessary to enter such careers. The belief that librarians are not particularly well prepared for technical work because of their general lack of technical degrees reveals an underlying misunderstanding of technical work. Systems librarians do need to achieve technical competence to perform their duties satisfactorily, but there are many ways in which to accomplish that goal.

These assumptions also lead to another challenge. Technical work is frequently elevated to the level of the magical; only trained wizards need apply. Ironically, those who perform these secret wonders are frequently denigrated as people who have to be kept in check more than others because they control the magic. This belief hinders effective organizational management, destroys staff morale, divides the profession, and complicates librarianship's ability to communicate with colleagues in other technical professions.

A reasonable conclusion from these observations is that when one views the people in technical positions within libraries as somehow flawed, one misses opportunities to see how their respective backgrounds can and do serve the organizations in which they work quite well. One also denigrates the value of having a widely diverse background, which in turn devalues all backgrounds.

The Structure of a Solution

These challenges notwithstanding, some solutions or remedies need to be pursued. Although these may not be easy to implement or may require a reexamination of priorities, they must be recognized as possibilities. The library profession must also begin to see solutions as multifaceted with joint responsibilities among library schools, libraries/employers, and students/employees. Despite the difficulties identified by Boyce and Heim (1988), the following items must be accomplished: (1) curricular adjustments, (2) multidimensional recruiting, (3) salary parity and adjustments, and (4) continuing education.

Curricular Adjustments

Many schools have already undergone significant changes to their library science curricula, revising traditional approaches to common topics and adding new courses to introduce students to important new studies and skills. Wallace and Boyce (1987) have outlined a sixth-year specialization approach for systems analysts. Despite the difficulty in getting students to complete further work with no guarantee of higher salary, this solution begins to address the need for additional preservice training. It is important to understand that this approach does not add requirements for all students; it simply provides a structured, formal opportunity for further advanced study. Similar examples exist in education, law, and medicine with postdoctoral studies, specializations, and subspecializations.

Multidimensional Recruiting

Recruitment efforts in librarianship from my perspective have been relatively abysmal. Open positions are usually advertised in local or national publications, preinterviews take place at professional conference placement centers, and occasionally library personnel staff will visit area library schools to inform graduating students of employment opportunities. More recently, libraries have advertised positions on Internet listservs or via Web pages. While these efforts may inform new or recent library school graduates who are already motivated and indoctrinated into the profession, they do not constitute recruitment—that is, bringing new people into the fold, perhaps ones who never considered a career in librarianship or who have some previous negative impression of the profession.

Therein lies the challenge of recruitment. This activity must take on a greater importance for the profession as a whole, not just for library schools. All current employees of libraries have opportunities to plant the seed in prospective recruits. Academic libraries particularly have an opportunity to foster interest in the library profession. All academic libraries employ student workers and have historically influenced many to later attend library school. Libraries with active systems units have a particularly good opportunity to recruit students with computer science, information systems, and engineering backgrounds. Now that employment opportunities also exist outside libraries for people who possess technical skills and an understanding of information organization and management (i.e., the training that librarians receive), the opportunities are great. Yes, it is difficult; yes, it takes time; and yes, it's usually one-on-one conversation, but it works!

Libraries and library schools must also look toward developing internships in library systems units for library school students who wish to receive hands-on training in a real systems environment. Many medium-sized and large libraries have developed sophisticated information systems and provide an arena of operational and management expertise that would benefit current students.

Salary Parity and Adjustments

The salary issue perhaps represents the greatest challenge because of constraints, both real and perceived. Fundamentally, the library profession adheres to a value system that emphasizes service and democracy. There is no need to apologize for those values, but there is a need to recognize that these values inform and influence the approach taken to compensation. In general, librarians do not wish to pit salaries against collections or access, all of which cost money. Nor do librarians wish to differentiate greatly specializations within the field. These concerns and budgetary constraints, size and classification, limit what can be accomplished in the short-term to bring library salaries up to parity with other similar positions.

Salary minimums have improved, although in some areas significant work remains. The profession, however, must continue to demonstrate, through successful improvements, a desire to compensate its members adequately. In any area of responsibility within a library, but particularly for technical work, added duties must be accompanied by added incentives, one of which is salary. Braeg Epstein, reporting from a 1990 Dynix survey of system administrators, quotes one respondent to the question of change in salary, compensation, or status upon assumption of system duties, "dream on!" (Braeg Epstein 1991b, 56). Such a response does not reflect well on librarianship and is likely to limit successful recruitment of technical personnel. While it is true that salary is not the only motivator for employment—and given professional values, librarians probably would not want it to become so—work must continue to develop pathways for improved financial remuneration for systems librarians.

Continuing Education

Another incentive that can motivate technical personnel is a demonstrated commitment on the part of the organization to ongoing continuing education. While librarianship has demonstrated through its professional societies, consortium arrangements, and network affiliations a significant commitment to continuing education, most of the content has been focused on nontechnical material or technical material that is appropriate for all librarians, not systems people specifically. This pattern follows what has occurred in library schools.

Librarians employed in systems units, or working in systems-like positions, frequently require more in-depth training than is available from existing "library" sources. This need has forced many to seek out educational opportunities outside the profession, which in general is very positive. Establishing links with other professions not only broadens the perspective of the individual librarians, but it also provides opportunities to heighten the awareness of others to the interesting things happening in libraries. One caveat, however, is that these types of training tend to be more expensive than that provided within the profession. So, the questions become: how much should be invested in continuing education? And who is responsible for the tab?

The first question is not unlike the salary question. Based on my experience, some librarians are not willing to spend much on continuing education. For example, one state library association in the early 1990s was unwilling to charge participants more than $50 for a full-day technical and legal seminar on networking CD-ROM databases presented by experts from around the country. As a comparison, even the Fred Pryor training company charges $99 for a daylong session on customer service. The point here is that it costs money to provide valuable technical training; the profession is either willing to invest in it or it isn't.

The second question is always a sensitive one: who pays? On the one hand, continuing education benefits the individual and therefore should be seen as an investment in personal growth. On the other hand, the organization benefits from the increased knowledge of its employees and needs to offer incentives along with its stated expectations for continued growth. Support for continuing education is viewed by many as a significant employment perk. Although it may be difficult for a library to find within its budget significant new dollars for training, this effort must be made. Perhaps creative dollar-matching options with employees can be worked out or cooperative arrangements with other area libraries can be procured to reduce the overall training burden.

If a library already has money set aside for training, an additional concern is inadvertent discrimination of technical training in the form of dollar limits per session or flat-rate reimbursement. Because appropriate technical training will cost more than typical library training, policies and procedures that are based solely on traditional library continuing education will inevitably fail to address adequately this need.

Many sources of quality, high-level computing and networking training opportunities are offered by nonlibrary-related purveyors. Many of these provide traveling sessions that visit major metropolitan areas periodically. Some professional associations, both in librarianship and computing, sponsor such sessions as well. Opportunities also exist through formal coursework at local universities and community colleges. In addition, commercial training services that provide preparation courses for technical certification are a growing market. All of these are available at some cost. It is not unusual for a technical professional to require several thousand dollars per year in continuing technical education and development. In the language of popular psychology, it's time for the profession to have its walk match its talk.

One further note on sources of continuing education is necessary: authors and respondents to surveys have extolled the value of vendor-supplied training (Braeg Epstein 1991b; Muirhead 1994a). Vendor training can be placed into two categories: free vendor orientations or product updates and fee-based modular training.

The first category includes overviews and introductions to existing and new product lines that vendors inside and outside of the library arena typically provide at their sites, professional conferences, or meeting space in hotels in major metropolitan areas. Useful information about what a product is designed to do and how it performs can be garnered from these sessions—and a free breakfast or lunch, if one is lucky! Nonlibrary vendors frequently will work with local resellers to schedule these events so that multiple-related product lines that integrate will be represented at the same session. Question-and-answer periods and opportunities to interact with other current and potential customers add to the value of these sessions. The limit is that competitive options will not be discussed in any meaningful way; these sessions are a form of marketing, not comparative analysis.

The second category includes in-depth training on the use of specific product lines, both hardware and software. It is best represented by training that a library can purchase from an ILS vendor. This training is usually limited to topics on the design, use, and management of that vendor's system. Such training is very useful for a library at the time of implementing a system. Caution should be exercised in selecting an ILS vendor to provide training on topics beyond the system it markets (e.g., networking, Web design, or desktop computing). These vendors will represent their own worldview on computing that may or may not be in the library's best interest, or accurately represent state-of-the-art thinking on technical topics. Some vendor training is excellent and appropriate. The key to procuring effective training is balancing vendor- and other-supplied training, as well as free and fee-based options.

On-the-Job Training

In addition to finding a solution for formal preservice and continuing education opportunities, librarians must understand the tremendous value of on-the-job training. Surveys of systems librarians indicate that most have received the majority of their training on-the-job (Braeg Epstein 1991b; Leonard 1993; Muirhead 1994b). Boyce and Heim reflect negatively on this situation:

> It appears that the small number of librarians with strong automation skills, and the small number of computer professionals with knowledge of library operations, have both picked up their outside skills through work experience or by developing a strong personal interest in the problems of the other profession. This does not seem to be an ideal situation, but it is one that has worked well enough to produce most of our current automation professionals.
>
> (Boyce and Heim 1988, 71)

While the context of this statement is the then-perceived lack of appropriate preservice technical training in library schools and the difficulty in providing it, several assumptions exist under the surface of this expression that are worth noting. First, there is an implied suggestion that in an ideal circumstance on-the-job training would not be necessary. Or from another perspective, preservice education should be able to meet a complete set of training needs for all new entrants into a particular field, obviating the need for on-the-job training. One could easily argue that such a suggestion is unrealistic in any field of study, but especially in one that is as fast-changing as libraries or computing or one in which local system development or adaptation is so common.

Second, this approach denigrates on-the-job training by suggesting that it is second-rate to formal education in a field. This point further implies that expertise (i.e., knowledge and skill developed over time) has less value than degrees or certificates earned.

Third, library schools are assumed to be the best place to offer such training. Given the difficulties in accomplishing these changes in graduate education identified elsewhere in the same article and noted previously, perhaps alternative solutions might be a better course of action, or at least considering multiple avenues should be pursued.

The point is not to dismiss a particular article, analysis, or concern, but to recognize: (1) that on-the-job training should not be treated as a disability, and (2) when unspoken assumptions may cloud thinking on the matter. On-the-job training is not only a reality we must live with, but one that has been reasonably successful. Furthermore, the notion of "strong personal interest in the problems of the other profession" seems to be a very positive interdisciplinary approach to the challenge librarianship faces. How exactly would this be different from a reference librarian or bibliographer with responsibilities in biology seeking to become informed of the concerns of the other discipline? It is important also to recognize that currently many of the people employed in these positions actually do have both a strong library background and computing expertise gained from both formal and informal experiences.

Underneath the surface resides another assumption worth noting. Librarians seem to believe that life in other professions and business and industry is significantly different (read "better") in this regard. Education, training, certification, and other formal means of evaluating and placing people are challenges for all professions. Dividing responsibilities between preservice programs and continuing education opportunities, and between employers and employees, is a common difficulty. Librarians should expect no easier time of it than anyone else has experienced.

What Should Systems Librarians Learn?

As noted previously, a variety of options are available for systems librarians to receive training in relevant areas. But what are the relevant areas of study? Given the wide variance of responsibilities across libraries, it would be difficult to state absolute requirements with any great certainty. The following content items are based on the areas of responsibility discussed in previous chapters.

Content areas of interest to systems librarians include:

Basic administration and management

Library administration and management

Basic accounting and auditing practices

Communication (interpersonal skills, training, documentation)

Personnel management (unit, departmental, and enterprise issues; hiring; writing job descriptions; performance evaluation; promotions)

Project management (time management, coordination, group process, negotiation, tools)

Information technology management (methods, trend analysis, trade-offs, case studies)

Disaster planning and recovery

Ethics of information technology

Information policy

Specification writing (functional and technical, RFP process and trade-offs, case studies)

Contract negotiation

Computing industry structure and relationships (how things work, product development, marketing, sales, distribution, support, manufacturers, value-added resellers, integrators)

Statistical analysis (research process, report analysis, how to read the literature, statistical modeling)

Classification theory

Data structures (MARC and non-MARC bibliographic formats, metadata options, nonbibliographic options, relational structures, trade-offs)

Software/hardware engineering process (design process, case studies)

Operating systems

User applications

Programming (exposure to multiple-development environments, trade-offs)

Database design (structure, elements, trade-offs, outcomes, large-scale projects)

Information retrieval systems (design, management, bibliographic and nonbibliographic data requirements)

Integrated library system management (actually installing, implementing, and managing one or several)

Network architecture and management (actually constructing a network based on a planning and evaluation process)

Large-scale networking (enterprise-wide solutions, Internet technologies, design and service issues)

Network protocol analysis (history/development, case studies, interrelationships, trade-offs)

Security and authentication (concepts, implementations, trade-offs, case studies)

Physical plant management (electricity, HVAC, structural)

Principles of electricity and electronics

These content areas at first glance might appear overwhelming. How could a one- to two-year graduate program in library science ever hope to address all of these in addition to other important library-related coursework? A number of these topics could be addressed in single courses to bring the awareness and skill up to a level appropriate for a beginning systems librarian. In other cases the material might be incorporated into intensive short courses a week or two in length. As mentioned earlier, the responsibility for exposure to these content areas also does not reside solely with library schools. A systems librarian will need to seek deeper knowledge of relevant content areas once placed in a given context.

There is also a need to employ specific delivery strategies and teaching modalities in the presentation of the identified content areas. The following methods help reinforce approaches and attitudes critical to systems librarianship:

> Review and analysis (analytical, communication)
>
> Group projects (team building, cooperation, coordination, communication)
>
> Hands-on projects (cognitive transfer, process knowledge)
>
> Internships in live systems offices (demonstration, application)

Paths to Learning

The appropriate education of a systems librarian will be necessarily eclectic. People in these positions are called on to function in a variety of technical and nontechnical roles. To prepare students to face the demands of the marketplace, a wealth of educational opportunities must be afforded them. Library schools in general have begun to address the technical literacy of librarians as a whole. The time has come to make the changes necessary to meet the needs of this specialization. To succeed in this endeavor, library schools, library administrators and managers, professional associations, library consortia and networks, vendors, and individual librarians must begin to seek and support multiple alternatives for achieving the goal.

Whatever alternatives are identified or developed, they will cost real dollars. All concerned parties can no longer expect high-quality training and performance for little or no investment. It is antithetical to suggest as information professionals in the age of information that librarians do not require significant continuing education. Individuals and organizations will increasingly need to fund these growth opportunities. Muirhead notes:

> To sum up, the future of education and training of systems librarians . . . will be a continuous process requiring imaginative and creative solutions involving contributions, either singly or in partnership, from the various interested parties together with a commitment to [Continuing Professional Development] from systems librarians supported by their employers.
>
> (Muirhead 1994a, 100)

As with most issues in life, a sense of balance is key. On the one hand, librarians must not lose sight of the rich history of principles that libraries and library education engender in an attempt to fit with a fad. On the other hand, very real change has occurred in the ways that librarians perform their responsibilities. Creating and investing in opportunities to address these changes is wise.

4

Organizational Structures for Library Systems Units

It is true that without men there would be no cultural forms; but it is also true that without cultural forms there would be no men.

—Clifford Geertz,
The Growth of Culture and the Evolution of Mind

Few, if any, surveys address organizational structures for systems units, departments, offices, or divisions across all types of libraries (Muir 1995; Muirhead 1994b). It is possible to glean some information about organizational structures from job advertisements, but such sources are spotty at best and certainly not necessarily representative. Furthermore, the information that exists is widely variant, suggesting that libraries have been more responsive to local perceptions and available options than to profession-wide standards or prescriptions. In fact, profession-wide standards simply do not exist.

This topic could be approached from a variety of perspectives. In recent years, academic library literature has discussed the merger of campus computing organizations with libraries or the rise of chief information officers (CIOs) with technical and information resource units reporting through that line (Woodsworth 1991). This discussion will focus on structures for operational aspects of systems units within a library in general.

A First Look

Job titles are one way to uncover the diversity of positions, and to some degree, reporting structures. The following list of titles has been gleaned from position announcements relating to systems work in libraries or library vendors advertised between July 1996 and October 1997. These titles were selected because the positions had some significant level of involvement in systems work. They by no means exhaust the possibilities in the field, but illustrate the wide range of ways in which the library community classifies these positions.

> Associate University Librarian for Library Information Technology
> Automation Services Manager
> Computer Services Librarian
> Coordinator of Library Automation
> Data Administrator
> Desktop Systems Support Manager
> Digital Resources Specialist
> Head, Systems
> Information Technology Librarian
> Library Consultant
> Librarian for Digital Collections and Services
> Library Systems Coordinator
> Library Systems Head
> Library Systems Manager
> Library Systems Programmer/Microcomputer Analyst
> Manager Technical and Automation Services
> Network Administrator
> Network and Systems Manager
> Network Librarian

Network Resources Librarian

Product Analyst

Systems/Collection Management Services Head

Systems Librarian

Systems/Public Services Librarian

Technical Services Librarian

These titles reflect not only a desire to create interesting-sounding positions to attract candidates, but also an attention to local needs and constraints in combining duties and areas of expertise.

Position announcements also sometimes provide an indication of reporting structures. The review of these positions, in cases in which the reporting line was noted, indicated the following titles:

Assistant Director for Technical Services

Assistant Director for Technology Planning and
    Administration

College Librarian

Dean

Director

Head LAN/Personal Computer (PC) Management
    Department

University Librarian

These titles also suggest a wide-ranging variety of options in the field. To the degree that these findings are representative (a conclusion that is not statistically supported), it would seem that systems positions, despite the nature of the individual titles, report to positions rather high in library organizations. Foote's (1997) survey of position descriptions for systems librarians in academic libraries suggests a somewhat similar conclusion.

Muir (1995, 4) notes that among ARL members nearly all heads of systems offices report to either a dean/director or an assistant/associate dean/director/university librarian. The survey respondents indicate an increase as well in the diversity of titles given to the head of the systems office over this same period (p. 5). The organizational charts included in this publication support the notion that libraries—large academics in this case—structure their operations according to different needs and philosophies.

Evaluation of the Options

Evaluation of the effectiveness of different organizational structures for systems work is difficult for several reasons: libraries tend to have affinities for local preferences, perceptions, and philosophies; evaluation metrics are ambiguous and parochial; and few people wish to reflect poorly on their chosen structure.

Library operations with few exceptions have historically reflected the needs and desires of local staff and patrons guided by the beliefs of a director. Libraries, however, are also known for their sharing nature, both with regard to collections and operations. Countless how-to guidebooks and lists have been published, and some of the more active electronic discussion lists contain information of this type. Librarians have taken seriously the desire to avoid reinventing the wheel locally if at all possible.

The organization of systems units, or their existence at all, is a topic on which librarians have expressed myriad opinions. Some have extolled the virtues of having a systems office that answers to individual units within a library to keep them responsive; others have argued that the unit should be staffed with a minimal number of technicians and that high-level expertise should be developed throughout the other functional units within a library. The descriptive surveys conducted to date indicate that libraries have indeed put these opinions into action. Systems units are created, or not, and organized, or not, according to the diversity of opinions held in the profession.

Holding these differences to the flame of objective reason, however, is not straightforward. Certainly local needs do warrant variation, and the availability of funding and personnel budgets lines will greatly influence a library administration's decision. In addition to these pragmatic realities, it is difficult to assess how best to meet these needs because the needs themselves are frequently in contention, poorly defined, or misunderstood. Indeed, certain organizational structures may arise to avoid the difficult task of building consensus about such needs. Furthermore, the people working in an organization, particularly those who have made decisions concerning systems work, have powerful disincentives to admit publicly that something is not working. After all, changing a decision that was made based on one's beliefs requires the decision maker to admit that he or she was wrong or driven by popular trends.

Administrators have many incentives to create, or re-create, effective and productive organizations, but change takes time, often a long time, to permeate an organization. In the absence of documented evidence to suggest that one structure is superior to another, experimentation may appear the most appropriate vehicle for discovering the best solution. Few organizations, however, handle experiments in structural redesign well. This tendency is because, by its nature, this exploration implies a fluid design that is changed routinely based on feedback, while most people prefer some level of stability.

A review of any segment of library literature will reveal a strong preference for the how-we-did-it-good type of article, as opposed to ones that honestly document the misunderstandings, misreads, mistakes, and corrective actions. That is not to say that librarians are particularly prone to this fault; in fact, it seems to be a human trait in general. When considering topics such as this, however, librarians must recognize the limits of what information is likely to be available for evaluation.

Facing the Music

Position Classifications

One pragmatic facet of organizational structure is the use of position classification schemes. In addition to defining who reports to whom, these schedules identify advancement paths and levels of remuneration. Many libraries must use the classification schemes established by their parent organizations, which may or may not adequately deal with a number of positions common in libraries. This circumstance may limit the flexibility libraries have in dealing with systems unit structures.

For some, technical positions may need to be shoehorned into library position classifications. For example, a library technician in one department might perform binding repairs, while in another might install and troubleshoot computers. Not only does this potentially limit appropriate advancement within the organization, but it also inadequately differentiates responsibilities and prerequisites and ties these positions to library-based salary schedules that may not reflect market realities for technical positions.

To accommodate the need for technical expertise and to attract suitable candidates, some libraries have made technical positions management-level as well, thus increasing the overall salary range for a position. While this approach can work in the short-term, it creates several dilemmas. First, if a computing person is in a management position, presumably he or she is supervising someone else. That responsibility takes away from hands-on technology work, which is presumably what the library is paying for in the first place. Second, while it might be possible to have the person report to a different department head to alleviate some of the management burden, earning more than one's supervisor can create some problems as well. Third, there are likely to be some other equity issues among library management positions to resolve. Fourth, such a strategy tends to concentrate expertise at the top of an organization, which runs contrary to the way organizations actually achieve goals—expertise needs to be shared and pushed down and around the organization.

In-House Expertise

It is sad, but true, that libraries in general tend to pay less than many other industries for comparable positions, particularly in technical fields. In contrast to this situation, real expertise costs, and libraries do pay for it in one way or another. Some libraries do pay at or near prevailing salary levels for technical positions and hire technical people in the market. Other libraries develop expertise in-house and pay for it on an installment plan. Although the latter option may appear less expensive, hidden costs may exist such as longer project implementation times, inappropriate decisions based on inexperience, or time away from other projects—for in most in-house development programs systems duties are added to existing responsibilities. Wide variances, however, stem from a combination of factors.

Building expertise in-house is not without its challenges. For example, it can be very expensive to send staff to appropriate training, and without it many would be floundering. Once knowledge has been gained and hands-on experience follows, the expertise that has developed is highly marketable. It will cost to develop, maintain, and retain a trained and experienced technical staff.

Outsourcing

For some libraries the solution may lie in contracting out the need for certain expertise. Academic libraries may be able to receive the support they need from an information technology (IT) division on campus, or public libraries may find suitable expertise in another city or county office. Commercial firms also provide technology support services.

Outsourcing certain functions has been popular in business and industry for a number of years. IT and IT support are commonly outsourced. Teaming up with an experienced third party to handle workstation implementation, software support, hardware and software upgrades, and network management is believed to be an effective way to manage the cost of IT. To the degree that support and service can be discretely defined, they make good candidates for contractual relationships in which expectations for quality of service are outlined. One prime attraction for outsourcing is that the arrangement provides a flat-rate budgetable cost item for these services.

Libraries have outsourced a variety of services for years (e.g., approval plans, binding, serials subscriptions). IT could be another successful option. While some businesses have been generally successful in achieving their goals through outsourcing IT, it is worth noting that a number of larger companies are reconsidering the option, citing unmet expectations in vendor expertise, focus on core competencies, quality of service, cost, and transition to new technology. Some of these companies are rebuilding their in-house IT staff; others are renegotiating new contracts with shorter time frames and less broad goals (Caldwell and McGee 1997). The issue is not so much that outsourcing is completely inappropriate as it is that significant planning and consideration need to precede the decision.

Providing IT support, whether acquired through buying the expertise, developing it in-house, or contracting for it, is a challenge. For most libraries, the options are limited, but decisions need to be made in light of these identified issues with the full awareness that a perfect solution does not exist, and local considerations may well determine the success of a particular option.

Model Principles

Given the lack of specific evaluative information, the variation in the field, and the challenges of developing or buying technical expertise, perhaps the most productive approach to the topic is to identify basic principles on which structural design details should be grounded. I recognize the danger in prescribing specific solutions for all libraries, so the following recommendations are given in the spirit of defining issues that must be discussed locally prior to evaluating a current design or setting the course for the future. It would be wise as well in this discussion to separate structural issues from position descriptions and from personality traits of current or past employees. The intent is not to state that some library is doing it all wrong or that others have it all right. That will remain a local issue.

Centralization

The first issue to address is whether or not to centralize the systems functions. Jaffe (1991) vehemently argues against centralizing these functions and expertise. His argument, however, fails to recognize the efficiencies and economies of scale that central management can afford. In fact, many businesses are returning to centralized management of IT resources after years of pursuing a distributed model. They cite "easier management, lower costs, improved security, easier disaster-recovery procedures, increased performance, and simpler storage strategies" as reasons (Garvey 1997a, 64). Woodsworth (1991, 19) also notes that as information technology brings together previously unrelated areas within academic institutions, some level of coordination, a centralized function by its nature, is necessary.

Other factors must be considered as well. For example, centralized support can offer a more consistent level of service and deployment across an organization. Departments that do not have expertise in certain technical areas or that do not have loud voices still have computing needs that a central advocate can address. Perhaps the most important point to make in this discussion is that centralized service and support does not imply the lack of departmental expertise. In fact, the two can and do coexist.

While the mileage will vary for each location, the following items are benefits of a centralized systems division, peopled with appropriate staff:

across-the-board technology training—minimum
   competencies

centralized efficiency

consultative support

contingency planning

coordinated project development

coordinated technology planning

dependency cross-checks—no one flies alone

enterprise-wide communication

information technology resource management

matching needs and resources organization-wide

security and risk management

service to the whole library—balancing needs

standards for hardware and software

standards for support and documentation

On the one hand, I cannot hope to convince those who are ada-mantly opposed to central systems units. On the other, perhaps some will begin to see that this situation is one that is filled with trade-offs. Indeed, in any area in which there is so much variation, one should expect to find trade-offs that individual sites have decided by design or by default they are willing to accept. In general, the lack of centralized service and support can lead to the following neg-ative consequences:

duplication and inefficiency

inability to share some types of information electronically

lack of coordinated reporting

lack of coordination on computer projects

low responsiveness for smaller units

more professional time spent on low-level computing tasks

uneven technology adoption—haves and have-nots

Detractors will note here a lack of turf and control issues. The reason for this absence is that these issues are not structural; they are based entirely on personality. Certainly such traits impact the effective operation of a unit, but they will influence a distributed operation in the same fashion as a centrally organized one. Furthermore, systems people do not have a corner on such traits, they can be and are present throughout organizations at all levels within administrative structures.

A key factor in the success of any systems unit, no matter how it is structured, is communication both within the unit and with other units in the library. Perhaps many of the difficulties encountered with technical units in one way or another reflect poor communication. Centralized systems units offer the opportunity to protect the information technology investment a library has made while maximizing the availability and stability of the resources.

Evaluation

To ensure that a unit is functioning appropriately, it must be evaluated, as should each person within it. Perhaps most of the concerns of those who are "anticentral" would be addressed if they felt systems units were held accountable for their responsibilities and actions. Systems units wherever they report must be responsive to the needs of the organization and its constituents. The feedback gained from other units can be used to improve operations.

Reporting

Libraries vary significantly in the administrative location of technology or automation units. Some have the unit reporting through the technical or bibliographic services division; others have it reporting through access services or circulation; and still others have it reporting to the director. Nearly every conceivable option can be found.

As with most things, there is no single right way to do it, but one major factor should be considered in designing the reporting lines: representation. At what level should computing resources and planning be competing? If everyone is satisfied with the deployment, perhaps it is not an issue. In some cases, however, having a unit that serves the entire library reporting to just a part of the library could create some challenges and political fallout. Another question to ask is: how strategic is information technology? The answer to this question may suggest the appropriate reporting line for a particular library.

Teams versus Hierarchy

Recent management trends in business and industry, as well as in libraries, have highlighted the value of project- or function-oriented teams of workers who are responsible for identifying solutions, making decisions, implementing options, or managing operations. In general, teams are thought to capture more effectively the expertise of the group, improve overall communication, and encourage personal ownership of projects and functions. Moreland (1991) notes the positive impact that shared responsibility for microcomputer support can have in getting staff to own their expertise.

Popular and more scholarly treatments of the changes occurring in society indicate a tendency to flatten organizational hierarchies in an effort to improve involvement and communication to create more flexible and competitive organizations (e.g., Drucker 1988; Peters 1992). Business models that emphasize flat organizations have had an impact on libraries, too. Gorman (1987), for example, believes that academic libraries need to focus all staff on service, remove hierarchies, grant autonomy, and reorganize interdependent functions.

While the focus of this chapter is the organization of systems offices, the general trends in library administration and management are relevant to the topic. Systems librarians must be aware of and participate in reorganization discussions for they will be impacted by them. Likewise, other people who participate in making structural decisions must understand that the need for systems support and services exists independently of the organization of both the unit offering the service and the library as a whole. They also must understand that the outcome of the debate between teams and hierarchies does not preclude either outcome regarding centralization or decentralization of technology management. In other words, a library can decide to build an organization that is team-based *and* centralizes its IT management, just as one can maintain a management hierarchy while distributing technology responsibilities. Systems librarians can and do function in teams, hierarchies, and interesting combinations of the two styles of organization.

In seeking to reorganize a unit, department, or enterprise, decision makers absolutely must know what issues or problems are realistically expected to be addressed by the change. Failure to recognize the fundamental difference between structures and personalities can thwart the intended benefits of a change. While one can argue that personalities are influenced by other human structures, one cannot ignore that personalities are a factor in any human organization. Anyone who believes that a structural change by itself will magically reform the occupants of the organization is naive. Personalities are persistent.

If one expects structural change of any kind automatically to eliminate inefficiency and division, one is misguided. An organization that has a relatively flat structure can suffer from these ills, just as one that has an identifiable hierarchy can seek to value human input, creativity, and decision, as well as operational efficiency.

The fundamental point that must not be lost in the midst of decisions about library organizational structures is that the need for technological expertise and support exists within all libraries despite respective beliefs or decisions regarding the best approach to management. Structural designs do not guarantee that some things will happen and others will not. They can create safeguards and methods of monitoring progress toward organizational goals and away from nonessential activities—in short, accountability. They also do not directly determine the level of organizational input into processes and projects; they only provide opportunities for that. Much of the effectiveness of a particular design will, in fact, depend on the willingness of the organization's members to make it work and to adjust according to ongoing evaluation.

Recommended Design

For the reasons discussed previously, I highly recommend a structure for library systems that reports to the library director and participates in all senior administration discussions or team-based decisions within the organization. Systems work increasingly permeates all library operations and functions. It is appropriate that this specialty be present at a high level. Martin (1988) notes:

> In order to be a full contributor to the evolution of library services, the systems librarian should report to the library director, who should stimulate rather than squelch or ignore new ideas and initiatives. The location of the systems function within technical services is a holdover from the early days of library automation, and is a structure that also cannot respond adequately to the challenges of today and tomorrow. (pp. 59–60)

This position should oversee an operational department that plans, implements, supports, trains, and experiments for and with technology. The size and structure of the unit will depend on the size and needs of the local library. This unit should operate under administrative mandate to serve all units within the library with regard to technology, assisting them as necessary in carrying out their respective missions in the most effective way by employing appropriate levels and types of technology. The systems unit should also seek to develop or encourage the development of technical expertise throughout the organization.

As an aside for those who worry about technocrats determining library directions, perhaps involving systems personnel in more library discussions would assist in improving the understanding of the issues by those who do not already understand them and thus address any local concerns or performance problems. Systems personnel in general, and systems librarians in particular, have demonstrated throughout the world that they are capable of understanding and serving library needs admirably. In fact, several former systems librarians are now directors of major libraries.

5

Technical Management

Life's a dance you learn as you go;
Sometimes you lead, sometimes you follow.
—John Michael Montgomery, *Life's a Dance*

Systems librarians manage a variety of technologies employed in libraries. This responsibility includes not only handling the installed hardware and software, but, in many cases, also entails supervising other technical staff. As in other areas of this specialty, balancing human and technical issues is imperative.

What Is Technical Management?

Much of the composition of technical management is similar to management in other units within an organization. Providing a productive environment, setting goals, prioritizing demands, removing barriers to success, pruning unwieldy projects, and representing needs to administration are all parts of strong management in any specialty.

Technical management presents some differences, however. First, because technical staffs tend to be smaller than those in other library units, managers are more likely to have "line" responsibilities in addition to oversight and coordination duties. For example, it is not unusual to find a systems librarian, who is part of a library's senior administration, debugging code and creating user accounts. The demands of these different levels of responsibility are significant for systems librarians, thus creating dual roles.

Second, while supervising technical staff has much in common with this function in other areas, some variances exist, at least in style. Good management, regardless of the people supervised, seeks to rally the talents and skills of the members of the unit toward meeting organizational goals. On good days, with highly motivated individuals, this experience can be inspiring to a manager. At other times, the responsibility can be enormously challenging. Several general principles can help meet that challenge. While these issues may be useful for management in other areas of libraries, they are essential for the operation of a technical unit.

Managing a Technical Staff

As mentioned previously, human effort and input are resources that become part of the organization's pool. While all staff have much to offer, some may require more attention in getting them to recognize what they can contribute. Seeing technical staff as a valuable resource empowers a manager to match talents and skills with projects. At the same time, demonstrating an appreciation of that value provides a morale boost even in the midst of high demands.

Believing that staff has value, however, is not enough; showing them is what counts. A technical manager must consider not only the organizational needs and departmental resources when assigning tasks and projects, but also other factors such as departmental constraints, timelines, recent past projects and their outcomes, the perceived nature of all current projects, an individual's current project load, learning opportunities, and personal preferences. Without this additional input into decision making, a manager is doomed to alienate technical staff. Considering these factors does not guarantee success, nor does it mean that everyone does only what he or she wants. As with many issues in technical management, it is a matter of thought and balance.

Operations and Exploration

People who choose technical careers are likely to value exploration and experimentation. In a technical work environment it is important to feed this value in some meaningful way—it is an asset. Technical staff who have opportunities to explore new technologies can discover creative ways of dealing with the day-to-day challenges of normal operations. Certainly, this need must be bounded by the requirement for operational services that are primary to a library's function. Both approaches can be united into a powerful combination that produces exceptional, forward-thinking support. Without some investment in this experimentation, an organization will most likely experience one of three outcomes: technical staff will become mired in operational grunge, their creative light snuffed; these people will find ways to explore on their own with no benefit to the library; or the technical staff will simply seek other employment.

Ownership in Projects

Technical projects are frequently thought to be easy to modularize into component pieces that get sewn together at the end; this approach is usually disastrous. One effective way to build competence and confidence in staff and accomplish departmental goals is to delegate whole projects as opposed to just tasks. Many systems units are so busy meeting the demands of other staff and users that it is easy to get lost in the shuffle and lose sight of the accomplishments achieved. By assigning responsibility for whole projects, or at least discrete components within a larger project, the individuals involved then have the opportunity to develop some sense of ownership or partnership in a process. Never underestimate the value of having staff buy into the goals and projects of a unit, department, division, and organization.

Professional Development

All staff need to refresh and retool from time to time, and systems staff are no exception. Formal opportunities to learn new skills or examine new technology should be encouraged and supported financially. In addition, development that focuses on less technical aspects of work, such as interpersonal communication skills, should also be facilitated. By advocating on behalf of the technical staff for these activities and by demonstrating support through personal commitment to these same goals, a manager substantially influences his or her department.

Leadership and Focus

Any area of a library risks ineffectiveness if the manager loses focus. Leadership demands a sense of mission, goal orientation, task familiarity, discipline, and human awareness. There has been much written on how to say "yes" and achieve win-win situations (e.g., Fisher, Ury, and Patton 1991). While it is important to understand human motivation as it relates to wanting to win, it is also important to recognize when resource limitations do not permit committing to a project without overextending a unit or risking loss of quality in other areas. These situations are the "tough" decision points that technical managers face.

For a department, however, it is absolutely critical that the members trust the manager to represent their talents, skills, and time appropriately in light of a variety of factors. Understanding departmental member's perceptions of the current environment, current performance levels, and the intensity of other current demands are all important observations for a manager. These factors must be balanced with the relative importance of a new request. Sometimes, "no" or "not at this time" would be the best response. Such an answer can return a department to its intended focus and ensure appropriate distribution of scarce human resources.

Visibility

Staff that work behind the scenes can become invisible to others within an organization. It is the responsibility of a manager to make them visible. Perhaps some of the best ways to highlight the work, and the value of the work to others, are in meetings, by memos and news bulletins, on Web pages, or with announcements. Get the word out on the street about what the people in the systems department are doing to help other units in the library or to provide new services for the public. Offer introductory information about the staff in the systems unit so that others can begin to become acquainted with them. This very basic information-sharing function is the foundation of ongoing professional and personal relationships.

Advocate for Needs

Once technical staff are visible, managers need to represent their needs to senior administration. This function is no different than for other staff. Not only does this accomplish securing resources for the unit, department, or division, but also builds trust between the manager and the employees that the manager understands the value and care of employees and will act on that understanding.

Salary Parity and Equity

One important need in most library positions is a continued commitment to improving the salaries and wages of employees. Parity and equity are two metrics in evaluating pay scales. Parity compares salary and wage data within a position grouping across industries; equity compares salary and wage data within an organization or unit. Technical positions within libraries have notoriously paid below market value, and it is unlikely that libraries will ever on average compete with some other industries. Be that as it may, this factor should not become an excuse to avoid accomplishing whatever improvements can be made.

Administrators must realize that it will cost a premium to hire qualified technical staff, particularly if one is seeking significant applied experience in a market where librarians now have other employment opportunities (Budd 1990). Financially attracting technical professionals with reasonable experience is likely to be difficult. According to *Network Computing*'s 1996 survey of network and information systems managers, the mean salary for these positions was $57,690 (Schnaidt 1997). This average compares more with 1996 director salaries at $58,297 (Lynch 1996, 25) than with what would be expected for systems librarians.

Equity issues are a matter of being internally consistent. If a library is not generally increasing salaries and wages over time and is increasing minimum hiring values, trouble is lurking on the horizon—compression. The goal is to ensure that the organization is truly paying for experience and relative contribution to the organization, not just responding to some bureaucratic oversight or loophole to reward newer employees at the expense of current hires.

Performance Evaluation

For some reason, performance evaluations appear to overwhelm many managers and staff. Perhaps the reason is that the evaluations are viewed as negative motivators or ineffectual tools for staff management. In a nutshell, these vehicles provide an opportunity for the evaluator and the one being evaluated to ponder and then discuss what has occurred over the past evaluation period, typically a year. But more than that, they also offer an opportunity to set goals for the coming period and outline the development objectives for the individual and the department.

In my opinion, performance evaluations are both overrated and underrated. Alone, performance evaluations do not create an effective department, nor do they guarantee a certain level of aptitude, skill, or dedication on the part of an employee. They are simply one tool that a manager has to document one picture of an employee and to communicate officially in a limited sense the value that the organization places on that individual's contributions. This tool is limited to the vision, talent, skill, and training of the manager.

On the other hand, performance evaluations can accomplish a great deal. It is possible to engender a trust relationship by ensuring that no negative surprises happen during such an evaluation. Technically there should be none, as any problem areas should have been identified and documented at the time of the occurrence or shortly thereafter. The opportunity to discuss candidly the areas in which an employee would like to develop, change, or improve overwhelmingly outweighs the challenge of evaluating current performance. A manager who does not take advantage of this opportunity is denying the employee a growth experience and himself or herself one of the joys of management: seeing people stretch and develop.

Certainly "problem employees" present a challenge, and not all employees respond positively to the same factors. In the case of poor performance situations, however, documenting the circumstance, and providing the opportunity for the employee to document and respond, is not only wise to support resolution, but also legally required. This documentation process can identify influential factors involved in a particular performance difficulty. I believe that under most circumstances responsibility for less-than-adequate performance is multifaceted, involving the employee, the manager, other employees, administration, and the organizational culture and context. Correctly applied evaluation measures can assist in identifying effective long-term resolutions.

Training and Development

Much of the material presented in this section assumes that technical staff (and managers) are appropriately trained. Preservice education and training are dealt with in other areas of this book. Here the focus is on the relationship between the performance of technical staff and how well they are acculturated into an organization. Part of this process takes place over a long period of time as the values of the organization and the individual interact and become internalized. A major portion of the acculturation, however, is also directly attributable to initial and ongoing local training. A new employee must be introduced to the organization and be informed of expectations—this should have begun at the time of the interview—as well as opportunities for growth within the organization itself.

Ongoing training that relates to a person's responsibilities is also necessary. The material covered must include not only how-to aspects of a job, but also the why-we-do-it-this-way perspective. In addition, depending on the nature of the responsibility, training may include the level of changeability for tasks. As mentioned earlier, giving responsibility to individuals for projects or tasks entails letting them discover creative ways to change the current order of things. Helping them understand the history of previous decisions will illustrate the constraints that must be considered when contemplating a change.

Accepting "Futzing"

The "futz factor" in computing is widely documented in personal experience and institutional lore. Stories range from the humorous to the disastrous. In its most basic definition, "futzing" is playing around with a technology to get it to work as needed or to improve its operation—tweaking so to speak. Given that computers are not yet self-maintaining organisms, the value and limitations of futzing must be understood and accepted for an organization to implement successfully this technology.

On the one hand, many would argue from personal experience in their respective organizations that systems workers should be constrained in their ability and rights to experiment with hardware and software. This attitude stems from negative experiences in which production systems have been inadvertently compromised in some fashion through tinkering or valuable time has been expended on work that may not be a library priority but is seen as really "cool." On the other hand, many systems workers would argue that without such experimentation a technology will not be understood, fully utilized, appropriately tuned, or correctly repaired. This approach has developed over years of experience, suggesting that no technology or product works as advertised right off the shelf. Thus, "futzing" with it is absolutely necessary.

There is no direct resolution to this conflict of ideas. Success in negotiating this disagreement requires balancing needs and expectations, increasing understanding on the part of the proponents on both sides of the issue, and improving overall communication. Much of the disagreement reflects a naïveté on the part of everyone toward the position, needs, and circumstances of the people on the other side. A common belief of participants arguing for restraint is that computer systems actually work as proposed right out of the box or that documentation and vendor support will suffice for any changes needed during implementation. Understanding this belief, incorrect though it may be, helps to illustrate the level of frustration experienced when changes occur on the fly, implementation is delayed, or the system is down for modification.

On the systems side of the debate, some believe that users have overly inflated expectations, lack sophisticated experience, and remain rigid and inflexible. With this view in mind, it is nearly impossible to entertain seriously the needs of users when contemplating change, exploring problem resolution, or implementing new systems. In most cases, people are not intentionally aiming to harm or inconvenience others. If that is the case, then there are other management issues that need addressing. In fact, what is happening here is a complete lack of communication. The people in these two camps of thought are not even using the same language or lexicon; and therefore, they have no hope of building partnerships and trust until these issues of understanding each other are resolved.

Technical staff need to understand that when users of a system express their needs and concerns, even in the presence of an all-too-common technical naïveté, the issues raised are valid. Part of systems work is to develop an understanding of what users need, even if the "why" is not completely shared or accepted. It is equally important for systems staff to appreciate that perception is just as important as system functionality. If users perceive that system managers remain behind closed doors issuing proclamations regarding the system, no matter how technically proficient the staff is or how technologically advanced the system is, trouble is brewing. Users require accurate and timely information regarding the operations of systems and sensitivity to nontechnical factors in planning for change and downtime.

Users, in this case primarily library staff, for their part need to recognize that technical problems are frequently complex and not solvable in three simple steps, that computing technology entails balancing trade-offs, that there is no such thing as 100 percent uptime, and that not everything is documented. Having a technical staff that is willing and able to experiment to find a resolution to problems and to improve the performance of systems is an organizational resource beyond compare. Such a resource should be managed, not eliminated.

In situations where understanding and trust do not exist, the first step is getting people to talk with each other, even if at first the language presents a challenge. Establishing guidelines together for how to handle known circumstances is a good benchmark that, if followed, will engender trust over time. Understanding that many circumstances will not be known ahead of time is also necessary, but addressing the known ones consistently will improve the resiliency of the organization in handling the unanticipated.

For managers and administrators, particularly in large organizations, it is worth noting that providing resources so that experimentation can take place in the background provides a start for accomplishing the goals of both sides of this issue. Users can work in a more stable environment, and systems staff have a separate context for testing and learning. The organization benefits enormously.

Understanding the Technical Mind

Technical managers must understand what motivates technical staff, how they are likely to approach things, and what communication style they are likely to use. Not everyone employed in technically related work thinks or acts the same or is motivated by the same incentives, but there are some orientations that are common to people drawn to this type of work.

One area in which tensions are common is in communication styles. For example, when problems are reported, technical staff are oriented toward fixing the problem and will be seeking relevant details on the symptoms of the problem. If the nontechnical person reporting the problem insists on diagnosing the problem rather than describing the symptoms, the technical person is likely to get frustrated. It would be as if a patient visiting a doctor were to respond to the question, "What's wrong?" with the answer, "I have appendicitis," rather than, "I have lower abdominal pain." Likewise, the nontechnical person is likely to be offended by the technical person telling him or her that he or she doesn't understand the technology.

A technical manager must remain aware that these tensions exist and will arise from time to time. Technical staff are neither always in the right nor always in the wrong, but they do need to be supported in matters that assist them in performing the duties for which they were hired.

General Principles

A variety of issues relate to technical management that defy classification. They are presented here as general principles.

Thinking at the Enterprise Level

One of the most important, and yet most challenging, elements of technical management is keeping the enterprise in mind at all times. Enterprise-level thinking informs all decision-making processes. This approach entails an awareness of the interdependence of all activities and projects in one form or another. It also suggests the need to involve diverse groups of people in the process of planning and implementing new systems and services. This way of thinking emphasizes the importance of implications, consequences, and relationships.

All technical managers must possess, or develop on the job, the ability to function in this fashion. It is somewhat related to focusing on the forest as opposed to the trees. It can be learned by actively engaging the organization in the process and remaining open to understanding how an organization operates on many levels. This approach to technical management may suggest particular ways to structure an implementation, such as the introduction of a new integrated library system. Or it may highlight feasible options for ensuring data and system security throughout an organization. A way of thinking such as this is not one thing, or even one set of things; it is a process that influences all other management functions and principles.

Managing for the Default

Managing a situation or circumstance without much thought or preparation might be called management by default. Most people probably would agree that such a style would not constitute proper management. For one thing it does not imply any level of responsibility or conscious decision making. Managing *for* the default, however, is a completely different approach.

Implementing most technologies entails making a variety of decisions regarding parameter settings, naming conventions, user restrictions, colors and layout, among many others. These decision points are common, but they do have implications for how a technology or device operates and how easily it will be managed over its life span. In many cases, the choices revolve around which options will be default values and which will require special attention. When establishing a default value for user disk space on a new file server, it makes sense to set the initial value at a level that is common to the most users on the server. By doing that, the exceptions are minimized and more easily managed.

The same type of approach can be taken to a variety of management tasks in systems work. Any time there is a need to deal with the resolution of a multifaceted set of problems, discovering a change that will address the most aspects and dealing with the exceptions individually saves time and effort, as well as money. Managing in this fashion requires a keen sense of what solutions may address outstanding issues, an awareness of how interdependent many things are, and a willingness to negotiate effective resolutions despite what might appear on the surface of the problem or request. Techniques such as this are necessary for there are not enough hours in each day to deal with all problems and requests individually. Some may require special attention, but if that approach becomes the norm, soon efficient time management goes out the window.

Differentiating Possible and Feasible

Possibility and feasibility routinely get confused or misused. Stating that something is possible in technical terms means that someone has done it or that the technology exists so that it can be accomplished. In other words, it can be done. Feasibility is much more complex because the concept implies the inclusion of other factors related to the circumstances under which implementation might occur. For example, the amount of money one is willing or able to spend, the length of time one is willing or able to invest, existing infrastructure, contravening technical factors, conflicting goals, and other political constraints, among other issues, all determine to some extent whether or not something is feasible.

In carrying out technical management responsibilities, a systems librarian is likely to hear about how some other site is doing x, y, or z at times when a request for x, y, or z is denied. The implied assumption in situations such as these is that possibility and feasibility are the same thing. Just because something works a certain way at one site does not mean that it will be the same somewhere else. There may be many factors to consider—many of them nontechnical.

Knowing When to Say "No"

In an environment that includes groups of highly motivated people who wish to accomplish great things and are committed to quality service, it might seem slightly contrarian to suggest that an individual must be able to turn down a request. With regard to human and technical resources, however, situations do arise in which requests for service, special attention, new projects, adds and changes, etc., must be evaluated in light of competing priorities.

To understand the nature of this challenge, one must consider the notion of opportunity dollars. For projects that require the purchase of new physical items, most librarians can understand that sometimes there is simply no more money to be found in the budget; thus, a prized project goes back on the shelf. Staff time, however, also costs real dollars, although they are frequently not the same as the dollars used to purchase furniture or computers. These dollars often are referred to as opportunity dollars in the sense that if a person does not do a particular task, the organization does not recoup those dollars; the person still gets paid and receives benefits. On the other hand, the organization has the "opportunity" to redeploy that individual's time and effort toward another project, task, or duty. These dollars generally cannot be easily adjusted, but they can be shifted from priority to priority.

It is also important to understand that limits exist on what an individual can accomplish within a given period. For example, there are 24 hours in each day, there are certain required activities in the course of a day (e.g., eating, rest-room breaks, mental and physical shifts of focus), and most positions do require some interaction with other employees. While it may be true that some people are more efficient in their use of time, statistical limits to efficiency would suggest that after a certain point the goal becomes counterproductive. (See Stephen Jay Gould, *Full House: The Spread of Excellence from Plato to Darwin* [New York: Harmony] for clear explanations of statistical boundaries in a variety of common and scientific areas.)

Furthermore, efficiency is one of those entities that is in tension with other attributes such as quality of work, complexity of circumstances, and importance of detail among others. That is to say, if one were to concentrate solely on maximizing efficiency, these other attributes would suffer. Seeking balance among all relevant attributes should be the goal.

This discussion can be summed up in the simple statement: when one decides to do one particular activity, it likely means deselecting some other activity. Some activities can be performed in tandem, and other activities can be assigned lower priorities that imply completion at some point in future time. The inability to select and deselect or prioritize activities that consume opportunity dollars constitutes a major threat to the efficient use of professional—or any other—time and expertise. Despite what popular management fads may suggest, every professional must be able and willing to say "no." To do otherwise does not get one to "yes," it merely indicates a blatant disregard for available resources. And in the case of management positions, it is not just a matter of burning oneself out, it includes derailing an entire organization.

Maintaining Communication

As discussed elsewhere, communication is a critical component of technical work. It warrants a high level of attention from technical managers. Both within a unit and with external departments, fostering and maintaining open and productive communication channels is important both for effective technical work and for creating and preserving positive perceptions of the services rendered. A technical unit cannot survive without devoting resources to this important element.

Building over Time

In this day of "So, what have you done for me today?" attitudes, it is difficult for professionals to concentrate on longer-term goals and accomplishments. Difficult, yes, but necessary! Being the flash in the pan for an organization provides some level of immediate gratification both for the individual and the others in the organization and may even stimulate positive public relations. But critical to the survival of the individual and the organization is staying power. Demonstrating not only an ability to grasp opportunities, but also a knack for sustaining development and improvement over time is absolutely necessary for technical professionals. A new system, feature, or service may be cool, even valuable, but its importance, measured in a time frame longer than nanoseconds, will be determined by its relative stability (i.e., accessibility, availability, and consistency), integration into the here and now (i.e., fit with existing tools and environments), and perceived added value.

A common underlying element of these factors that influences the importance of new things is infrastructure. Unfortunately infrastructure is not glitzy and does not generate intensity, unless, of course, it fails. Focusing on the foundation on which services are offered requires stamina, persistence, and discipline. Many forces are at work to erode support for infrastructure. For example, deferred maintenance on physical structures in libraries has freed up money for other more exciting pursuits . . . or has it? It is difficult to provide a working computing cluster that encourages the exploration of electronic resources when the roof is leaking rainwater on the computers and users. Or perhaps network design was done "on the cheap" to divert dollars to expensive monitors on the workstations, but now performance is so slow that users complain constantly. It takes guts to build sustainable resources over time in a fashion that the organization can support, both technically and in terms of service.

In the midst of this incremental approach to resource management, opportunities may arise for substantial leaps in improvement.

Along with managed growth, these spurts of innovation can be balanced. Risk-taking approaches should be encouraged among all staff, but real risk taking implies being there for the accolades as well as the fallout. Doing so builds confidence in the systems and services offered. Whatever the circumstance, the goal is to be responsive both now and in the future.

Understanding Scalability

Scalability, the capacity of a solution or option to adapt to and accommodate growth in any related factors, is widely misunderstood. This concept is not inherently a technical one, although it is frequently a factor in technical discussions. The decision to check all outgoing handbags and backpacks manually at the door of the library to reduce the amount of theft is a solution that may work for smaller or less-trafficked libraries, but it may not scale for larger or heavily used ones. With regard to technical solutions, perhaps the popularity of home computers and consumer electronics devices has influenced the mistrust of professionals arguing for specialized hardware and software that tends to be more expensive than off-the-shelf options. Often the reasoning for specialized computing equipment is based on the notion of scalability. Will an item be able to accommodate the level of anticipated use and expansion? In determining the appropriateness of a particular solution, the following factors must be considered:

Experimentation versus production

The nature of a particular project must be clearly articulated. If a library is experimenting with a new technology—or one that is new to the library—a small pilot project may be in order. On the other hand, if the new system is to support 100 users in production mode, a different approach would be wise. In the former case, a less powerful option may make sense for it would place fewer resources at risk should the project prove untenable. For some sites, however, it might be wise to consider the relative likelihood of success in the pilot and plan for a solution that could easily accommodate a production load once the details are known. In the latter case, the demands of a production environment are typically different than those experienced in experimentation. One is not necessarily more demanding than the other, but they do differ in nature. In fact, some laboratory work may be accomplished on a completely different platform. An awareness of the project goals and details, as well as a sensitivity to the existence of technical variances in products, is required.

Size really does matter

The capacity and speed of the central processing unit (cpu), the amounts and types of memory, the capacity and types of disk drives and other storage devices, and the design of the network interface all contribute to the overall performance and applicability of a particular computing solution for a task at hand. While it is useful for a systems librarian to be able to mold the technologies already in place, readily available, or inexpensively procured to address particular needs, it is frequently counterproductive to expect solutions to fit circumstances for which they were not designed. Certainly, more resources should not be expended than are necessary, but knowing the appropriate limit a priori is often difficult, if not impossible. The details of configuration and capacity influence other factors, too, such as performance, reliability, and longevity, in addition to scalability.

Flexibility and manageability

It is worth noting that the notion of scalability includes the idea of flexibility. Once a solution is in place, can it be modified to reflect changing needs? Or is it so specialized that it cannot be modified? For most libraries, change of some degree is a constant; this factor should influence all technical decisions. Technical solutions also need to be managed, that is, maintained and monitored. Particularly in the case of networking equipment, the less expensive options do not support management features. For smaller and more controlled environments, having this capability may not be so important as it is for larger, more complex, or less controlled networks.

Home versus office computing

The home computer market and the consumer electronics industry have brought computing devices of one type or another into most homes in the United States. The expanded exposure to computing in the general populace is helpful from a training perspective, but it has also influenced some approaches to institutional information technology in not so positive ways.

Some people believe that a computer is a computer is a computer. The only difference, once you decide on features, is the price.

In general, for home computing there is probably a large grain of truth in that belief. For office or institutional computing, however, other factors must be considered. For example, most home computer users are not using their computing devices constantly for eight or more hours per day; in institutional settings that type of use is common. Most home computer users are not connecting to one or more networks; office users do. Most home computer users use commercial, off-the-shelf software exclusively, while institution computing frequently entails the use of locally developed programs.

Furthermore, for libraries, public computing is very common. (See also Chapter 6, "Gotchas, Myths, and Parables of Systems Work," "Public Computing.") Public computing is different from both home and office computing in significant ways. The wear and tear on the equipment is substantially higher because more than one or a few users use the same machine, and it is in much more constant use than in any other environment. The impact of anonymity should also not be overlooked: whose machine is it? The lack of direct ownership or responsibility for a unit by the user influences the treatment of the device. Public computing in libraries has more in common with automated teller machines (ATMs) and interactive museum displays than with home or office computing.

Keeping the Eggs Out of One Basket

Libraries sometimes fall prey to overdependence on a single vendor. Given the importance of the integrated library system in the library technology pantheon, it is common for that vendor to be granted a special status. Other databases are mounted on that system, opinions on networking and remote access are sought from that vendor, and technology training is provided by that one vendor. While for some libraries the ILS vendor may be the only option, in general it is wise not to depend so much on any single vendor for technology products and services. If it is absolutely necessary to contract with just one company, it should be a conscious, justifiable decision. Although libraries can do well in outsourcing a number of services, responsibility and accountability should never be contracted out.

Establishing Feedback Loops

Effective technical management requires the creation of adequate evaluation mechanisms. These feedback loops provide input into the perceptions toward the service and performance that a unit offers. Without them a technical unit will become isolated and ineffective. Knowledge of technology as well as the organization being served is a critical component for feedback loops, but communication and openness are key to success. Meetings, both formal and informal, as well as e-mail and other "real-time" vehicles can provide input into the evaluation process. Customer opinion surveys can also be useful. The results of these ongoing processes must be sorted, selected, and prioritized for affecting change and improvement. Moving in this fashion requires a strong belief in the value of this input and commitment to responsiveness.

Most important in establishing these mechanisms is the willingness on the part of the technical unit to adjust and remake itself in response to the feedback received. If the use of these devices is strictly for lip service, people will quickly cease offering useful responses.

Learning on the Fly

Despite the value of preservice education and prior experience, technical work demands an ability to learn as one goes. No one will know everything from the start; the universe of knowledge is too broad, and change is too persistent. Functioning in this environment often requires a seat-of-the-pants approach that discomforts some people. Certainly some learning can be planned, just as many projects are known in advance. Systems work, however, does require a comfort with learning based on immediate need. This reality reinforces the need for conceptual understanding that can be particularized as needed. Thus, having a unit populated with quick studies is a valuable technical resource.

Knowing Strengths and Weaknesses

Any strong service organization survives because its members have an honest, accurate sense of strengths and weaknesses. The technical manager must maintain this mental image of self and the others in the unit. No one is perfect, but that fact does not need to create barriers to success. Individually and corporately, technical people need to build on what exists; there is no other way to move forward and improve. It also helps to understand the needs of the organization being served. To affect improvements in these areas, however, a manager must prioritize goals for change. In this age of the "change is inherently good" philosophy, organizations can easily become unstable because of unfocused, literally constant fluctuations. In fact, not all balls can be up in the air at once or continuously. Focused change is effective change.

Documenting What Is Done

In the fast-paced world of systems work, documenting procedures and decisions is frequently left to later. It can be a time-consuming task. Perhaps some would argue that immediate action on new requests for service outranks that need to document or that anyone in the future should be able to figure out what was done in the past. (Make that argument to someone who has inherited an undocumented network and watch the response!) While it may be true that emergencies demand immediate attention, routine requests should not automatically outrank knowing what has been done and for what reasons. As for being able to figure things out in the future, much time can be wasted attempting to surmise what someone did in the past, what implications or constraints were involved, and what problem was being addressed. Effective technical management entails establishing consistent procedures for documenting procedures and decisions.

Grounding Activity in Mission

Sometimes technical staff and managers get it backwards and emphasize activity as opposed to accomplishments that relate to mission. In today's fast-paced mode of operation, many people suffer from glorifying activity. It seems every person and each organization is expected to be on the move constantly—activity for the sake of activity. F. Scott Fitzgerald once said, "We run faster and faster trying to catch up with a past we have irretrievably lost."

Phenomenal energies are invested in covering the reference desk, cataloging the Internet, reducing the lines at the circulation desk, specifying the fastest computers, procuring greater network bandwidth, extending the hours of the branch libraries, ordering new materials, checking in new issues, updating Web pages, reshelving consulted or returned items, reviewing company X's latest database offering, teaching users how to operate the online public access catalog (OPAC), answering *that* question yet again, getting the bathrooms cleaned, helping a student with a science project—a neverending stream of activity. None of these things are unimportant or inappropriate; indeed they must be done.

Once in a while, however, people in an organization must be reminded that these activities are not disparate entities, unrelated to something larger. Activity without purpose is empty. Indeed, these activities must grow out of mission. When people busy themselves with such activities to the point of losing sight of their respective missions, vision fades, purposeful energy wanes, and they are at risk of being sold someone else's vision or splintering into chaos.

Building Coalitions

Successful projects frequently entail involving partners in the process. In some cases, because of the breadth of a project, input and involvement may be politically necessary; as a matter of standard operations, it simply makes good sense. Involving people with the parts of a plan that they can support creates an environment of collaboration rather than one of competition or antagonism. It is also wise to note that coalitions create and enhance the sense of community among those who share "a life and a task in common" (Hanson 1997, 42). Common ground can be found that adds value to the endeavor and purpose to the activity. (See also "Strategic Alliances and Partnerships" later in this chapter.)

Maintaining Technical Competence

One steep challenge for technical managers is fostering technical competence in themselves and in their staffs. Preservice and continuing education issues are dealt with elsewhere in this book. In addition to those expressed needs, the technical manager must understand that as management functions and roles become more prominent in his or her responsibilities, new skills will be required and less time will be available to focus on one's own technical competence. Thus, the nature of that competence is likely to change. The focus may become more broad rather than deep—or as deep as it was previously. A manager, however, must ensure that the depth of competence is maintained within the unit as a whole (Durham and Kennedy 1997, 182–183).

Planning

The secret to planning is seeking a balance between the significance of the endeavor and the investment in the planning process. For example, a library that is considering a new building or a new ILS should spend significant amounts of time in planning and preparing for the project. On the other hand, selecting a new spreadsheet product or the color of brochures describing the online catalog would not warrant such an extensive investment. Some general principles should be kept in mind.

Everything costs

The most costly portion of planning—or not planning—is time. The time spent on one process cannot be reinvested in some other process. Thus, the decision to enter into a planning process and to determine the level of activity required should be taken very seriously.

Nonlinear process

Much of the planning process revolves around attempting to look into the future and discover the most advantageous route to pursue. The planning process, however, can be sidetracked when the participants, or some of them, believe that the future can be known. In fact, with regard to technology, any projection beyond four to five years is likely to be either wishful thinking or relatively vague in its content. In either case, the prognostications are highly susceptible to the preferred future of the prognosticator. Care should be taken when making significant decisions based on sets of assumptions.

In addition, the process of making technological advancements is not linear and does not lend itself to analysis that assumes movement from point A to point B directly. Other factors always influence the discovery process and the marketability options for technological developments. Thus, extending the vision with implied certainty beyond what is now known is risky business.

Risk exists

Death is the only option for eliminating all risk. If librarians wish for libraries and themselves to continue to exist, it is more productive to recognize that every option includes a level of risk. Some projects may involve little, or less significant, risk, such as changing the paper used for certain reports. In this case, if the library has done it before, the likely challenges are known and can be assessed. In other projects, such as migrating to a different integrated library system, the risk level is much higher and greater consequences could develop if projections are inaccurate.

Risk, however, can be known and managed. First, however, the planners must understand their own comfort—or discomfort—with the various levels of risk associated with any future outcome—or the projection of a particular outcome. Then a discussion can ensue concerning known and unknown factors. Best guesses will do under some circumstances, but only if the planners understand how these relate to their level of comfort. Comfort with risk has much to do with the relative optimism or pessimism the individual possesses. Organizational culture also influences risk-taking behavior.

Formal process

Planning can proceed along very formal lines that include tools such as systems analysis, whether or not the options considered include automation and computing. Formal systems analysis can be useful for large-scale projects that encompass entire organizations or entail huge expenditures. Despite both overly positive and overly negative reactions to the process, "systems analysis is neither a threat nor a panacea; it is simply a valuable tool under many circumstances for identifying and solving problems, including commonplace problems facing library administrators" (Osborne and Nakamura 1994, 1). "Systems analysis . . . remains merely a technique: a means to an end. It is based on applying rational and logical methods" (p. 2). "It is not, however, a panacea or a magic bullet. When it is applied with cynicism or indifference it can produce grotesquely distorted results . . . Perhaps even more dangerous than cynicism is worship" (p. 21).

Before embarking on such a process, Osborne and Nakamura warn that a problem must exist to warrant such an investigation. They identify four necessary components to determine the existence of a problem that can be addressed through this process: alternative options, a decision maker, doubt about the best solution, and a context for interpreting its nature (1994, 34–35). Without these components, it is doubtful that sufficient focus can be garnered to resolve the problem using systems analysis.

Some authors suggest routinely applying these types of quantitative analyses to the management of technology in libraries (e.g., Clayton 1992). In many cases, such a process is warranted; in others, it could be overkill given the nature of the real decision at hand. Furthermore, all structured planning grows out of a context with a given set of assumptions that are perhaps unconscious: (1) life is quantifiable, and therefore everything becomes an object; (2) complexity and ambiguity can be reduced; and (3) objective methods can minimize subjective influences. All too frequently, systematized planning when applied to information technology is significantly flawed precisely because it does not address the following truths: (1) there is no perfect system, platform, vendor, software package, network topology, etc.; (2) many evaluative factors employed in analysis lack agreed-on measurements (e.g., ease of use); and (3) the very outcome the process seeks to avoid—subjective opinion—is, in fact, an integral part of effective and efficient computing.

The case for planning:

> orderly
>
> efficient use of resources
>
> balanced objectives and outcomes
>
> relationship to organizational mission
>
> opportunity for range of inputs and perspectives
>
> avoidance of common pitfalls

The case against planning:

> too rigid
>
> inefficient use of time
>
> too much invested in process, not enough in outcome
>
> risk of getting someone else's solution
>
> balance is a ruse—only balances articulated issues
>
> encourages abstract mission statements
>
> no spontaneity—inability to respond to change
>
> miss opportunities to learn—some things can't be
> known in advance

There is middle ground, however, in stressing the importance of planning and understanding the contexts within which decisions are made. Balancing the investment in the process with the nature of the problem at hand is key. At times, analysis and planning on the fly may be the most appropriate method; this would be akin to the barroom-napkin method. Planning in general, however, particularly organizational strategic planning, has garnered significant interest. The title of a recent editorial perhaps best summarizes the concern many have regarding strategic planning, "Plan or be planned for" (Riggs 1997).

Purchasing and Total Cost Analysis

Purchasing

Common opinion holds that personal computers are commodity items only differentiated by features and price. This notion comes mainly from purchasing units that want to save money for their respective organizations and vendors that wish to compete in the market. Both positions are understandable if somewhat misguided.

In many organizations, but particularly public ones, increased pressure exists to avoid sole-source purchases (i.e., items that must be purchased from one and only one vendor). The theory holds that by creating functional specifications (rather than technical ones), the experts on the functional side (i.e., librarians) can state their needs, and the experts on the technical side (i.e., vendors) are free to suggest ways in which their products can meet these needs. In some cases, this approach actually works, but more by luck than by design. It assumes that the vendors actually do understand library needs and the technology they sell and that the librarians do not understand or need to understand the technology. With the kind of work libraries do, many times the librarians are truly both the functional and the technical experts. Vendors generally do not like to be called to task on their expertise in this way. (Please note: this is not an indictment of all vendors, just an indication of an approach that does not work well.)

The bid process is also designed to provide for three important issues: best option, least cost, and avoidance of favoritism. While the bid process does have its downsides, these three reasons are cause to keep at least a portion of it, keeping in mind that any human process can fail to meet its objectives from time to time. With these concerns in mind, a systems librarian can construct solid technical specifications for computing equipment in a fashion that provides for competition and results in the library receiving what it needs.

The following are two examples of technical specifications for a microcomputer:

Example of Loose Specifications

> Pentium processor
>
> 32 MB RAM
>
> 1.2 GB hard drive or larger
>
> CD-ROM drive
>
> Windows 95

Example of Tight Specifications

> 233 MHz Pentium II or faster
>
> Phoenix or Award BIOS dated no earlier than 1995
>
> 512 KB Cache
>
> Memory
>> support for at least 128 MB RAM directly on the motherboard via 72-pin SIMM sockets
>>
>> 32 MB RAM installed in configuration 2 × 16 SIMMs
>
> Motherboard design
>> at least 2 ISA slots, with at least 1 slot capable of holding a full-length expansion card
>>
>> at least 4 PCI slots
>>
>> no after-manufacture defects on motherboard
>
> Drives
>> 1 2.1 GB (or larger) hard disk drive
>>
>> 1 16X (or greater) CD-ROM drive
>>
>> 1 1.44 MB, 3.5-inch floppy disk drive
>>
>> 1 100 MB Zip drive
>
> Video card
>> PCI bus
>>
>> at least 4 MB video RAM
>>
>> support for resolutions up to 1280 × 1024
>>
>> if video circuitry is embedded on motherboard, disable must be possible

Monitor

    SVGA compatible

    .25-mm dot pitch or smaller

    Trinitron tube

    support for resolutions up to 1280 × 1024

3-button trackball

Windows 95, at least interim version ###, including documentation, CD-ROM, and Microsoft certificate

All systems must undergo 48-hour burn in

3 years parts and labor depot warranty

All components must be new; no rebuilds, refurbishes, or returns accepted

If any specifications are not met, vendor will assume responsibility and cost of returning merchandise

While there is never any guarantee that any system a library receives will function over the course of its life exactly as planned without intervention, tight specifications will improve the likelihood that the library receives something that serves its needs. Without them, vendors are free to supply whatever they see fit to offer.

This same approach can be used for other computing and networking purchases. The extent of the specifications, however, should match the total cost of the deal and the complexity of the project. For example, an RFP for an integrated library system could be hundreds of pages in length; such a document for ten microcomputers would be overkill.

Total cost analysis

To understand how this approach to purchasing pays off for a library, it is necessary to consider the total cost of a system—whether microcomputer or other—over its anticipated life. At this point in microcomputer technology, the average useful life of a computer is three to five years, and that period is shortening. To find the system total life cost, sum the original price and all maintenance, upgrades, repairs, and ancillary costs. The outcome is the total life cost of the system. While this level of analysis could be done for each machine individually, such a job would consume hours of time and still would not reflect the actual cost of computing in an organization.

So, another procedure is used in business to assess this cost. Sum the total organizational expenditures for information technology–related items, including staff and training expenditures, and divide by the number of systems in place. Although this approach equalizes all machines on the average, it does give a good picture of the real cost of computing. It also heightens one's awareness that individual purchasing decisions do significantly affect the organization's total investment in technology.

A good way to illustrate this impact is by considering the purchase of some less expensive microcomputers from a nonmainstream vendor. In all honesty, it is a risk. For some sites, the initial saving is worth the increased risk of system failure and repair costs over the life of the system; for others it is not. It is worth noting that even the mainstream computer vendor products have failures. The point is not to suggest a single solution; the point is to make an educated decision. Most reputable vendors will respect, and even appreciate, knowing they are dealing with an educated customer.

Some of the most widely cited surveys of information technology costs come from the Gartner Group. Recently the group's surveys indicate that the total cost of purchasing and maintaining a computer is $13,000 per year per machine (Gibbs 1997). At first glance this may appear inflated—and to some degree this reflects a difference between business establishments and libraries. With a little analysis, however, the figure can be put into perspective.

These surveys attempt to measure *all* the costs associated with the purchase, installation, maintenance, and use of the computer. This figure is derived from summing all computing personnel costs (salaries, wages, benefits, and consulting fees), internal and external training, maintenance and repair, upgrades, software, and network connections. In addition, they include the previously mentioned "futz" factor—the cost of the time spent by each employee trying to figure out how to get something to work or trying to help another employee figure it out. The original cost of the computer is amortized over three years and the other dollar values, because they are annually recurring, are added to the annual figure.

Libraries do not have a strong tradition of closely examining total cost of service. It is understandable, but such a history does not assist professional awareness of the real costs of computing. Here's an example of what such total cost analysis might look like for a medium-sized library with fifty full-time equivalent (FTE) employees and 100 computers:

Original cost of computer:	$ 2,400	
(amortized over 3 years)		$ 800
Personnel:		
1 systems librarian @ $32,000	$32,000	
3 systems support staff @ $22,000	$66,000	
subtotal	$98,000	
benefits (30%)	$29,400	
total		$127,400
Software/upgrades: $200/machine		$ 20,000
Hardware/upgrades: $200/machine		$ 20,000
Repair/spare parts:		$ 6,000
Training (any staff computing training):		
$300 per year for systems staff		$ 1,200
$50 per year for all other staff		$ 2,500
Futz factor:		
(Gartner suggests 5.1 hours per week per employee) assuming average hourly wage for all employees is $10 then		
46 (50 − 4 systems) × 5.1 × $10 × 52 weeks		$121,992
Total annual expenditures:		$299,092
Per-machine annual expenditures:		$ 2,991
Annual amortized amount per machine:		$ 800
Total cost per machine per year:		$ 3,791

These figures are not suggestions on what information technology should cost in a library this size. This fictitious library spends precious little on training and does not pay its systems staff market wages. To illustrate how the total cost scenario plays out without giving too many opportunities for the reader to opt out by saying, "Well, we don't spend anywhere near that amount!" the author chose figures that would represent a variety of libraries. Even with these lower-level figures, the per-machine annual cost is still at nearly $4,000. These types of analysis give one pause to consider the real investment libraries are making in information technology. In this example, the library is annually investing close to $400,000 on computing and that does not include any subscriptions they may have to electronic resources, networking-related costs, or other costs associated with an integrated library system such as software licensing and maintenance. An analysis such as this also suggests that a lower initial purchase price for an item that requires additional labor to install or maintain may not actually save the library any money.

Achieving Closure

In any technical project it is important to reach a point of closure. People must sign off on the completion. Rarely do technical projects go exactly as planned or produce products that work exactly as anticipated. While such an experience may frustrate both users and technical staff, understanding the difference between "perfect" and "functional" is critical. Sometimes it is more important to have a working system than no system at all.

Resource Management

One of the key issues involved in systems librarianship is resource management. In fact, much of what constitutes a typical day in the life of a systems librarian could be considered in one way or another related to this issue. Systems librarians are called on to make decisions or recommendations concerning the deployment of computer and networking equipment, services, skills, and functions. This responsibility requires familiarity with the nature of each of these areas as well as a solid understanding of the arena in which they will be applied.

Resource management requires a broad, macrolevel approach to operations and planning. From one perspective, it is a philosophy—that is, a set of beliefs, commitments, values, and approaches. This way of seeing things suggests a wide interpretation of both library and computing issues that takes into consideration needs and available options for meeting those needs—perhaps nontechnological options at times.

Inevitably, in this matching game there will be times when needs outweigh resources. In cases such as this, systems librarians must be positioned to help others in their respective organizations to prioritize needs and desires in light of available resources. Sometimes the answer to someone's request must be "no," but perhaps there are other ways to get to a satisfactory result through other means. Successful negotiation of resource issues depends greatly on the systems librarian's ability to hold this broad and deep perspective in the course of serving an organization.

While systems librarians are involved in direct service to a primary clientele, this group of people is most likely to be the other people who work in the library. This being the case, it is crucial for systems librarians to understand the importance of the services that these other people provide, even if the librarians don't completely understand or value them. In working with other units within a library (and for that matter with patrons), it is greatly beneficial to determine the relative priorities of the people requiring assistance or requesting service. Not only does the interpersonal interaction proceed more smoothly, but more effective resource management can be achieved as well, particularly with regard to the amount of time invested in responding to the request.

A fundamental aspect of resource management is the identification and definition of resources. Equipment, facilities, and money are frequently mentioned as resources in a systems librarian's arena, but applications, data, and human effort are also important relevant resources. External support and services can become critical elements for this approach as well. To manage these resources effectively, a systems librarian must understand how each of these categories of resources, as well as the items contained there, interface with the library as an organization. Who is using what equipment, applications, data, and services and how? How important are these elements to the operations of a particular unit within the library? Are they ancillary and "nice"? Or are they critical? How do interruptions of service affect units?

Because systems librarians are frequently involved in specifying and contracting for equipment and services, a knowledge of the relative importance within a library of each item and the quality and reputation of the item and its vendor will serve the library well. Specifying and purchasing equipment are in fact part of this resource management responsibility. When a particular piece of equipment fails frequently, it quickly becomes evident that more resources invested earlier in the process may have reduced the current drain on them. Time clearly is a human resource consumed in this example, but persistence and tenacity can be other valuable resources at times when a vendor or purchasing officer suggests alternative, lower-quality or unknown, risky options.

The systems librarian's responsibilities of this type are similar to those of other specialists. For example, a librarian from an interlibrary loan (ILL) department will take into consideration the total cost of an ILL transaction, including staff time, postage or telephone charges, library transaction fees, OCLC fees, etc., and the time frame of delivery, when determining the most appropriate source for a particular request. In this fashion, the systems librarian views the computing resources within the organization to achieve an overall effectiveness in the use of these things.

Certainly an ILL librarian with years of experience would not pore over each ILL request, spending hours determining the ultimate best source for it, because his or her time becomes part of the resource management equation. Such excess would not effectively deploy the library's ILL resources. In fact, an ILL librarian is likely to make the investment in establishing procedures and training an appropriate level of staff to handle these requests. Similarly, a systems librarian establishes guidelines and procedures for handling computing requests in an effective manner in light of available resources. Over time many of these decisions may become second nature; that is part of what is called expertise!

Defining Resources

It is possible to define resources tightly in terms of their initial and ongoing costs to the organization. Models are available for accomplishing this (e.g., cost-benefit analysis). Unfortunately, it is also possible to be excessive in creating these models and filling in the details, to such an extent that more resources are spent maintaining cost per unit of work analyses than are spent on elements of the mission of an organization! Fortunately, there is much middle ground. The goal is to generate an accurate sense of what the items or units of measure in each category represent in terms of cost and attributable benefit. For example, suppose a microcomputer costs $2,000 initially and $5,000 annually to maintain. With an amortized life of five years, this equipment resource costs $27,000 over its life span, or $5,400 per year.

Measuring attributable benefit is a bit more difficult because the metrics are fuzzy. The most common benefit cited for computers is increased productivity. The challenge is defining and measuring productivity. Some economic models have been applied to productivity, but the orientation of most libraries is significantly different than that of business and industry to such a degree that these models may not fit. It is possible, however, to illustrate some of the less ambiguous examples of increased productivity in libraries caused by automation.

For example, suppose a cataloger could perform manual cataloging at a rate of five books per day. With the addition of a computer and OCLC access, perhaps that rate increases to ten books a day. If the cataloger is paid $37,500 ($30,000 plus 25 percent benefits), he or she costs the organization $144.23 per day or $28.85 per book the manual way and $14.42 per book the automated way. Over the course of a year, the difference between the methods amounts to $36,075 ($14.43 × 10 books per day × 5 days per week × 50 weeks per year—he or she deserves a vacation). This is a simple illustration with many possible caveats (e.g., most catalogers perform other duties as well, copy cataloging is frequently done by nonlibrarians; other costs are involved in operating a cataloging unit that are less sensitive to technology investment, etc.). It is straightforward, however, to see that the annual cost of purchasing and operating the computer ($5,400, not including OCLC access and usage fees) is more than made up for in the $36,075 increase in productivity.

Illustrations from other units in libraries are less concrete in terms of productivity measurement. For example, in a reference department it is difficult to assess a per unit of production measure. One could use number of questions answered, but it is not clear that technology is the most influential factor in that circumstance. A different measure, however, is possible: added services. With the addition of computing to public services in libraries, new options became available. Libraries have been able to offer services such as database searching, e-mail and Internet access, customized bibliographies, and remote access. The costs of adding the services can be calculated. The challenge remains to determine the value of these additional services to the staff and patrons. Certainly these services are popular; some days that knowledge will have to do in place of a critically acclaimed data analysis.

One caveat to these analyses is that productivity is a relatively ambiguous metric outside of production-based industries. Information technology's contribution to productivity is a debated topic (Gibbs 1997). "[W]hile IT is likely to improve organizational efficiency, its effect on administrative productivity and business performance might depend on such other factors as the quality of a firm's management processes and IT strategy links, which can vary significantly across organizations" (Rai, Patnayakuni, and Patnayakuni 1997, 89).

Automation Reduced the Libraries Expenses

Unfortunately for many years some librarians have perceived library computing as a means to reduce the cost of operating a library in the form of reducing staff. There is no documented proof of this belief. In fact, there are examples to the contrary:

> In actual fact, there is little evidence that automation has reduced staff size. While it may have drastically downsized certain departments—most notably cataloging—in many libraries, this has not usually led to shrinkage in the library as a whole. More often, it has meant the redeployment of staff, with new departments emerging and others growing in size. At the same time, of course, the staffs of the larger libraries have been expanded by the addition of people specifically involved in technological applications. In the early days, it was often thought that such appointments would be temporary; once the library was automated, the need for those people would disappear. Instead, these temporary appointments have become permanent and the proportion of the staff dealing primarily with the application of technology has increased steadily in many libraries. (Lancaster and Sandore 1997, 1–2)

It is dangerous to place such a high expectation on automation; it is even more deadly to share this perspective with funding agencies and administrators of parent organizations.

Automating a number of library functions in a variety of fashions over the past three decades has accomplished three things in this area of discussion: increased efficiency, where efficiency can be gained; increased productivity, but it is difficult to ascertain the details; and the creation of new services. "By embracing automation in the form of computer and telecommunications technologies, libraries are now able to offer services that they were quite unable to offer earlier" (Lancaster and Sandore 1997, 2). Even in these three categories it is important for the reader to realize that they are not ends in and of themselves; they are part of the broader issue of resource management. Automation has not taken libraries beyond these three categories of accomplishments, and every indication suggests that the investments in computing and networking will increase, not decrease. The reduced expenses argument is false!

Strategic Alliances and Partnerships

In systems work it is highly unlikely that an organization will survive without assistance in one form or another from outside sources. Sometimes these alliances may be required as a part of the relationship with a parent organization. While it may be frustrating to work within the constraints imposed from outside, many partnerships can be productive and supportive.

Computing Centers, Information Technology Divisions, and Data Processing Units

Some of the most common partnerships for libraries are with computing services departments within a parent organization. Much has been written about the merger of libraries with these units in academic environments, but administrative merger is not necessary to create successful working relationships. Because libraries need computing support in the form of specification and purchase, installation and maintenance, and operations and management, this partnership seems potentially useful, particularly for libraries that are smaller or do not already have in-house support.

These types of units operate on a centralized model that affords an organization certain economies of scale for purchasing and licensing as well as general training and consultation. Some libraries effectively rely on this support. The details concerning who is responsible for what must be worked out in a fashion that each unit understands and that the administration supports. Once such an agreement is reached, the systems librarian can coordinate the services required of the outside unit with the services provided in-house.

It is common for libraries to outsource some services in this fashion while maintaining in-house support for ILS applications, specialized training, and bibliographic utility operations. Under many circumstances, this is a wise decision given the availability of resources.

City Departments

For many public libraries, strategic partnerships with other city or county offices and departments are crucial for effective operations as well as for political survival. Centralized purchasing, computer consulting, data acquisition and delivery, personnel, public relations, property management, and many others may be fertile areas for alliances.

Vendors

Strategic partnerships can extend to the commercial realm as well. Projects may interest both the library and a vendor in which each party may contribute and benefit. Librarians have an opportunity to directly influence product development in this way (Drake 1986). In relationships such as this, however, it is important to avoid several detrimental outcomes: conflicts of interest, inappropriate or unclear financial commitments, and uneven tangible gains.

Conflicts of interest are fodder for investigations of public institutions and therefore should be monitored closely. In general, these situations arise when either party is unduly influenced by unrelated factors or the decision makers involved in the process yield, or potentially could yield, personal benefit for certain decisions. For example, if someone who has decision-making authority for selecting a vendor owns stock in one of the companies bidding on a project, that individual would have a conflict of interest. Some cases are a bit more subtle; for example, should an employee accept lunch from a vendor? The policy details on these types of situations are usually spelled out in human resources handbooks, purchasing guidelines, or administrative policy manuals within organizations.

Some partnerships with commercial entities include expectations of certain levels of investment in technologies, products, or personnel. Nothing is inappropriate about such expectations as long as they are realistic, equalized, and specified. A library is not likely to be able to invest $3 million per year in research and development, for example. Nor should a vendor demand that a library invest $300,000 in goods and services, while only contributing $50,000 of its own. Whatever the agreement is, it should be clearly stated in writing so all parties are operating with the same understanding.

Vendors participate in agreements like this to create new products and increase market share. It is appropriate that vendors gain from their investment in this development. Likewise, libraries should also receive tangible gains for their effort and input into the process, otherwise it would be difficult to justify participation. The goal is to create a situation in which each party contributes something and receives something of value in return.

Consortia

Most libraries belong to some type of consortium: local, regional, national, or international. For some it might be OCLC membership, while for others it might be a multicounty system. Libraries have a long tradition of entering into consortial arrangements to increase efficiency (e.g., shared cataloging), to reduce expenses (e.g., centralized purchasing for large-ticket items), to improve access to information (e.g., shared catalogs and other databases), and to share expertise (e.g., training seminars). In fact, these arrangements are one of the best-kept secrets about libraries.

Resource Sharing

Resource sharing among libraries stems from the consortial arrangements garnered. Because of its significance, resource sharing warrants a separate section. In the past, resource sharing agreements among libraries tended to revolve around access to cataloging information that reflected the contents of the participating libraries' collections. By knowing what other libraries held, patrons would be able to request the needed items through ILL agreements among the participating libraries. This model has served library users exceptionally well. More recently, a similar model has been applied to licensing databases and electronic publications. Participating libraries are able to offer these resources to their respective constituencies at rates far lower than if they were to pursue individual agreements with publishers and producers. The savings can also extend to shared hardware, software, and support. The economies of scale for large consortia are significant for library resources and services (e.g., CICnet, Galileo, Illinet, OhioLink, TexShare).

Strategic Areas for Development

For all the work that has been done within libraries to create strategic alliances and partnerships, there are still some areas in which more could be done. These are areas in which systems librarians can play a role in identifying the possibilities, forging the relationships, and monitoring the progress. Primary candidates for partnerships are: (1) cases in which the labor or cost are substantial and for which there is a common need, (2) cases in which more political clout can be generated by larger groupings, and (3) cases in which only part of the needed expertise is present in any single organization.

Specifications

It is not unusual for writing technical specifications to consume significant amounts of time. In many cases, the needs of different libraries are similar, if not exactly the same, and there is no benefit in reinventing the wheel. For example, libraries tend to create lengthy RFPs to specify needs and desires for large integrated library systems. These tomes are already frequently shared from library to library in an informal fashion. Model RFPs and templates could be created that would streamline this process or provide guidelines to the issues that should be included.

Many other examples of technical specifications are needed more often than RFPs for ILSs. Desktop computers and servers, network hardware, photocopiers, etc., are all possibilities. The payoff is that not everyone would need to generate them individually. Perhaps some minor modifications would be needed to reflect local requirements. Shared technical specifications, however, do not replace the need for some local expertise in interpreting whether or not a particular vendor's product meets them. Perhaps the specifications and a list of vendors and models that are known to meet the specs could also be shared.

Contracts

Model contracts for common products and services would also be a candidate for sharing. These documents take time to create and require additional legal review in most organizations. Having a base document with which to start would be helpful, particularly for organizations that do not possess the staffing or expertise to construct an advantageously worded contract.

Group purchasing

Many libraries are already involved in some type of group purchasing arrangements. Some of them may not even know that they are benefiting from these arrangements. OCLC, for example, through its regional affiliates, helps libraries to benefit from group purchase of some equipment. In the case of computing and networking equipment, far more group arrangements could be pursued. Small and medium-sized libraries could enjoy huge financial benefits from the group purchase of some types of equipment. In fact, more recently for large volume purchasers, manufacturers are willing to offer discounts for multiyear contracts that guarantee a certain level of purchase. In cases like these, libraries joining together would not necessarily have to purchase all equipment at the same time. For larger libraries the potential value may be reduced because they may be able to generate significant volume on their own or may already have contractual arrangements with manufacturers through their parent organizations.

Resource licensing

As mentioned earlier, shared licensing is a growing area for libraries. Large state consortia, such as OhioLink and IlliNet, are providing significant value for their members through discounted resource licensing. There is much to do in this regard. For some time to come, opportunities will be available for libraries that share some commonality (e.g., geography, size, subject focus, type, etc.) to find resources that all would value. One area that is just beginning to be pursued is national consortia of libraries interested in specific publications or types of publications (e.g., *JSTOR*).

Support

Supporting computing and networking will continue to be a large expense for libraries. Much of the cost is hidden in personnel budgets. While some organizations have considered outsourcing or have already outsourced support, many more might benefit from such activities. It is increasingly important for librarians to recognize that a large portion of library computing and networking is exactly the same as business computing and networking. Given that fact, local and national service and repair companies will contract for different levels of service. Many libraries could contract directly with these companies, but consortia could also perform this service, purchasing it on behalf of members at a discounted rate because of volume. In fact, some ILS vendors are already doing a similar thing either by contracting for client support with a third-party agency (e.g., the ILS vendor Sirsi contracts with Nichols for support) or by offering the service itself through another division of the company (e.g., Dynix provides support through its parent company, Ameritech).

Some library systems units are actually designed in this fashion. The unit offers certain levels of service to other libraries for a negotiated rate. Large public library systems have led the way in this regard (e.g., the Houston Area Library Automation Network).

Machinery, equipment, and space

As libraries continue to struggle with budgets and computing needs grow, even for small institutions, a great need may arise for subcontracting enterprise-wide computing solutions in which whole operations are outsourced, including equipment, software, support, and space (Rush 1992). Another variance on this theme could be contracting to have a company manage the whole operation on-site, similar to how photocopying or food service is handled currently in some organizations. Given the advances in networking technologies, it is already possible to have the management of computing and networking resources, including backups, account maintenance, software upgrades, problem diagnosis, and network monitoring, performed off-site. In fact, companies offer some of these services now.

Library consortia could take the lead in providing some of these services or in encouraging like-minded librarians to pursue these kinds of strategic relationships. Many libraries cannot afford to set aside the physical space and staffing to provide substantial computing and networking services and resources, despite their growing need for such things. These shared plans can bring the cost to attainable levels while providing high-quality services not available to small shops. The financial burden can also be amortized over a number of years for it would be an ongoing service cost, not a capital equipment purchase or personnel expenditure.

These strategic alliances and partnerships are the lifeblood of library operations. Not all options, however, will suit all library situations. One major factor to consider in determining the appropriateness of a particular arrangement is whether or not such shared resources will truly reduce the expenditures a library incurs in that category of the budget. It is also important to ensure that if a library decides to outsource something, the function actually transfers to the outside agency. Some responsibilities have a way of remaining for a long time despite administrative intent.

Another concern in establishing contractual relationships is monitoring performance. Libraries have successfully outsourced functions for a long time (e.g., approval plans, serials contracts, photocopy services). One of the keys to success is having the arrangements spelled out and monitored for effectiveness. In the case of computing services and operations, it is important to recognize that they are more time-sensitive than many other functions within a library (e.g., more like photocopy services than approval plans). When a computer is down, users are unable to work and frustration grows quickly. To address this issue, contracts must include provisions governing response time and possibly for some amount of on-site staff and spare parts.

Ultimately, however, the true test of effectiveness is in the satisfactory operation of the service and in the perceptions of staff in other units throughout the library. Note that this element should be no different than if a library has an in-house systems unit on staff: they should be responsive and effective, too.

Directing the Symphony

Any significantly large or complex project has much in common with artistic performance. Much practice or exploration goes on behind the scenes in preparation for the event, the talents of a diverse set of individuals are needed to pull it off, someone must coordinate the disparate needs of the people involved and facilitate their respective contributions with an eye toward the successful completion of the event, and no matter what happens the show must go on. Such an analogy to technical management also highlights that there is always more than one way to accomplish a goal.

A technical manager must be able to clearly understand and articulate the purposes of projects, the expectations for performance, the subtleties in interpretation of specifications, and the time frame within which the goals are to be achieved. In addition, he or she seeks to apply the talents of many individuals toward a community goal in a fashion that encourages each to offer his or her best.

A Balanced Approach

All of these issues or methods related to technical management can be overstated, misapplied, or abused. Some technical staff may use these principles as a means to forestall implementation of a new feature or product or to discourage innovation. Such abuses, however, are a failure of application, not of method. They should be dealt with in the manner in which any performance difficulty is handled within a particular organization. The occurrence of misapplication does not nullify the sensibility of these management approaches.

In this review of technical management, it again becomes clear that systems librarians play very diverse and influential roles in the organizations they serve. Their preparation and ongoing development is critical to addressing these issues.

6

Gotchas, Myths, and Parables of Systems Work

I therefore claim to show, not how men think in myths, but how myths operate in men's minds without their being aware of the fact.

—Claude Lévi-Strauss,
The Raw and the Cooked

Many oversimplifications or misrepresentations exist in computing and networking that serve only to confuse the novice and to provide fodder for the expert. Any book attempting to prepare librarians for systems work or to enlighten management on the complexities of library computing must address these issues. The inclusion of the following items is based on years of experience with technology and people in which I have discovered reductionism and polarism. The former is common in circumstances in which something is sufficiently complex and not widely understood at a deep level; difficult concepts get simplified. The latter occurs in cases in which ambiguity surrounds decisions; choices become binary. People commonly hold strong opinions because no one wishes to make the "wrong" decision.

Great potential exists for proliferating simple, unambiguous explanations that, in turn, generate lore, semireligious convictions and less-than-adequate understanding. In most cases, the truth can be found somewhere in the middle, a balance between extreme positions. While this outcome may be less satisfying because it is unclear and situationally based, it is, in fact, more accurate.

Many of the details that follow can be used to argue multiple positions. Some readers may take exception to the conclusions offered, but they illustrate that systems work, and life in general is not always so straightforward as it seems. Perhaps this chapter will debunk a few myths, challenge a few assumptions, and assist readers in finding balance among competing approaches.

Single-Solution Ideology

The most significant myth in systems work is the belief that a single solution to a problem exists and can be found. This assumption underlies many disappointments and disillusionments. It also has been a root cause of much finger pointing after projects fail.

This ideology is problematic from two perspectives. First, it is based on the notion that every question can be answered, every problem resolved, and every inconvenience eliminated. Perhaps in a perfect world such is the case; in systems work perfection is seldom, if ever, achieved. While it can be productive to have technical staff internally motivated to seek creative resolutions to the problems at hand, it can be counterproductive mindlessly to invest scarce resources in an attempt to continue a solution search despite evidence to the contrary of its existence. Furthermore, in real life addressing problems often entails compromise and negotiation, a balance of competing needs, priorities, and resources.

Second, this approach to technical work suggests that there is one and only one correct answer to a question. Such a concept negatively impacts creativity, effectiveness, and cooperation by focusing on some unrelated, random, and unfounded belief. Under some circumstances, it may be possible to document how one solution fits better than another in a given context, but changing some of the variables in the context will undoubtedly impact the relative fit of a solution.

Keep It Simple (and Cheap), Stupid! (KISS)

Related closely to the previous myth, this modified KISS method can also present some challenges. In systems work it is wise to build solutions that are not unnecessarily convoluted. After all, people need to be able to use what is created and someone will need to support it. Thus, it makes sense to keep the clutter to a minimum, and then presumably the cost will stay in line as well.

The challenge arises from the truism that the world is often more complex (and expensive) than many think. In contrast to the KISS approach, sometimes technical projects are necessarily complex to accommodate user needs, data structures, system interoperability, and organizational politics, to name a few. To build a solution that does not take these issues into consideration is to create a useless waste of resources.

The basis behind the KISS approach is found in a philosophical principle known as Ockham's Razor named after William of Ockham. This principle held that a correct explanation for a phenomenon would necessarily be the simplest one, unfettered with needless complex postulations. While in philosophical discussions perhaps avoiding Byzantine flourishes is considered good form, in systems work understanding all the attendant variables and contravening relationships is absolutely critical. It is not good form to overspend on a project, but it is also not useful to oversimplify reality. Balance is needed.

The Myth of Change

Change is a topic addressed in practically every body of professional literature. Even the popular press in recent years has emphasized the pace and depth of change experienced in the latter half of the twentieth century. With this common element as a backdrop in popular culture, it is far too easy to assume that the current generation is experiencing change at a rate far exceeding the experience of previous ones. Certainly no one would sensibly argue that change is not a routine part of most people's lives. Nor would anyone attempt to state that the pace of scientific and technological change has not been significant in this century.

Suggesting that the current generation's experience outpaces all previous ones, however, ignores some historical facts and lends credence to technological determinism. Some scholars, observers, and business leaders are beginning to question the validity of the change argument:

Alexander the Great conquered much of the known [W]estern world in 10 years. Nearly one-quarter of the population of Europe died during the first Black Plague, which lasted four years. The great wealth machine of the Yankee seafaring towns lasted a generation, the Pony Express less than two years. World War II lasted about five years after the United States declared war on Japan. Each generation living during those times was convinced that the "rate of change" was the greatest the world had seen . . . A quick review of U.S. business history—or any history, for that matter— shows that the presumption of "an era of change like no other" is a false but comforting myth. Believing that your generation alone is facing a unique challenge is a hearty bowl of comfort when you are on a diet of misfortune.   (Durham and Kennedy 1997, 25)

The idea that life—and business—was somehow more stable in the past than it is today is a fallacy. Not only is it untrue, the fact is that the last 40 years of Western experience has been *more* stable than most previous eras. But stability is not the normal state for human endeavor.   (Durham and Kennedy 1997, 26)

Comparing today's rate of change with the early nineteenth century, Ambrose notes the relative significance of the advances made around 1840. People did not expect life to change, thus the impact was all the more jarring. He outlines the drastic shifts in the nature of mobility and communication: foot and horse traffic versus steam engine–driven travel and the telegraph versus mail service (Ambrose 1996, 51–54; Maney 1997).

While the advancement of the digital computer and ancillary technologies in the latter half of the twentieth century presents a fascinating array of changes in common life, more questions must be asked about the nature of these changes, both physical and virtual. Has the computer—and more recently worldwide networking—really changed what people do as opposed to just how they do it? And have these changes affected the vast majority of the world's population at a level that competes with mass death and destruction, civil upheaval, or invasive physical change? If so, do they exceed these?

It would be difficult to argue that the computer and communications developments of the past fifty years have not had a significant impact on the lives of a large portion of the population, but the question remains whether or not such changes have occurred at a more disruptive pace indeed, or has the intensity of consumer-oriented, capitalistic marketing hype influenced the nature of the debate? Perhaps the evaluation of such quantities of change will remain by necessity a subjective matter.

The Primacy of the Internet

With the fantastic popularity of the Internet, particularly the Web, it is easy to get caught up in the whirlwind of activity surrounding Internet resources and technologies. While the development of the Internet and recent widespread implementation of access to it is crucial for librarians to understand and participate in, this involvement should not overshadow the need for knowledge concerning other technologies as well. In other words, the Internet is not all one needs to know.

Furthermore, what does it mean to "know the Internet"? For some, it may mean familiarity with a number of resources and tools for accessing those resources; for others, it could mean awareness of various national and international policy initiatives. For still others, that knowledge includes understanding packet-switching technology and router configurations. The point is that the Internet is not just one thing; it is many.

Systems librarians must possess at least a modicum of knowledge in all these areas, including the tools, resources, and politics. Being familiar with those areas is necessary, but a detailed understanding of what underlies these services and capabilities is important as well. The ability to diagnose connection difficulties and service failures or to determine when a vendor is attempting to mislead the customer requires a depth and breadth of knowledge.

As important as the Internet has become for many libraries, basic computing and networking remains the "bread and butter" of library computing. It may be desirable to have a Web interface to the catalog and access to journals and magazines on the Internet, but what really determines whether or not a library functions in this technological context in the first place has more to do with fundamental infrastructure such as desktop computers; network architecture, cabling, and hubs; file servers; and integrated library systems than it does with Java-enabled applications. Certainly change is under way in some of the ways in which networks function and where the computer processing takes place, in addition to new ways of developing applications. Be that as it may, such changes do not yet—

and are not likely in the near future to—obviate the need for local infrastructure and expertise.

Many library schools have been quick to jump on the Internet bandwagon in terms of including courses that focus on Internet resources, tools, and technologies. While in general such a change is appropriate, it is important for preservice education in librarianship to include computing and networking fundamentals. After all, the Internet consists of a variety of computing and networking technologies. To overlook the dependencies would be grave.

In the rush to include Internet topics, the glitz of the new topics may have overshadowed the need for basic computing and networking literacy. I fear that in some cases decisions to preempt other materials in the curriculum in favor of Internet topics may have been done because it was thought that the Internet was easier to teach. If true, such changes in focus would be unfortunate for topics such as data structure, database design principles, and network operations and management are just as relevant in these Internet-crazed days as they have been in the past.

The focus on Internet-related skills has also contributed to the increased ambiguity of what constitutes technical skill. For example, many librarians consider HTML encoding a technical skill. The ability to create a basic HTML document today is just as important as being able to use a word processor. It is not a highly specialized skill; in fact, software tools are on the market that make this effort very similar to basic word processing. Not everyone needs to be able to construct complex HTML documents, but familiarity with the environment should now be considered basic literacy for most aspects of librarianship. Thus, if library schools graduate students who think that knowing HTML, a few good Internet utilities, and how to search with Alta Vista constitutes preparation for systems librarianship, someone has been fooled.

Sustainability of the Virtual

Over the past decade the term "virtual" has been applied to just about every imaginable object or environment. The word has become part of the popular vernacular in the English language to such an extent that people no longer question its validity or appropriateness as a concept being applied to some new nonphysical or antiphysical world.

Nearly everyone who has experienced electronic communication of one type or another (e.g., voice mail, videoconferencing, e-mail, Usenet News, Virtual Reality Modeling Language [VRML], etc.) understands that these technologies can overcome some physical limitations, provide entertainment, or support some types of group communication at reduced cost. There may also be some social and cultural barriers that the technology can eliminate. But such "virtual" encounters are not new, nor do they necessarily address the problems at hand:

> Virtual communities have existed ever since written language came on the scene. If one of the touchstones of cyberspace is that participants know each other only in an intellectually-constructed, non-physical world, then the emperors of the Roman Empire were citizens of cyberspace. They relied on a complex communication system to build and maintain relationships with leaders holding power at the far boundaries of the empire. The Roman senators certainly did not meet each one of their adversaries but constructed a relationship with them in Roman cyberspace. George Washington was a citizen of cyberspace, too. Every evening after dinner and brandy, he would retire to his office, boot up his word processor, load his cyberspace software, and continue a lifelong discourse with great philosophers, politicians, generals, and farmers all over the Western world, many of whom he never met and never expected to. In his case his word processor was pen and paper, his cyberspace software the world postal system. It worked quite well for him and still does to this day.   (Durham and Kennedy 1997, 53–54)

These authors also note the need to view such technological solutions in the context of human communication challenges that are not just physical constraints:

> As a new technology, [groupware] must represent an improvement on the eternal problem set of meetings. They are the same problems we have tackled since we began talking to each other and no different than the problem set associated with conventional meetings. Groupware's significance will become obvious as long as we do not fall in love with the siren song of the technology itself.
>
> (Durham and Kennedy 1997, 54)

In addition, no matter how virtual an experience may be, it is wise to recognize that the technologies employed in creating such environments are very physical entities. They require electricity (and perhaps cooling), they take up space, and they require physical intervention at times (e.g., rebooting, upgrades, backups, etc.). At this point in time, it is also necessary for the users of this virtuality to receive sustenance—and some other support services—from time to time. That is to say that the virtual environments available now are inextricably tied to a physical universe. Perhaps at some point in the future life will be different, but for now decisions about computing and networking and "virtual libraries" and other such manufactured environments must be based on physical principles.

Open Systems

Much has been written about the value of open systems. Many believe that requiring vendors to create open systems will reduce overall operational computing costs. This standards-based design approach has been touted as flexible and manageable. Who wouldn't want an open system? Like many other technological terms, open systems have been defined in about as many ways as there are vendors in the marketplace. There is the potential for truly open systems to offer flexibility and interoperability, but these advantages come at a cost—both financial and in performance.

To understand the pros and cons, one must first decide on a definition. Is it hardware-based or software-based? Is it a matter of just the operating system? Does "open" imply no proprietary components at all? Must it run under Unix? Is it solely an interface issue? The debate is quite wide-ranging and at times confusing. In simplest terms, open systems are ones that provide documented modular interfaces at various levels within the total system, including hardware and software according to published standards. These systems potentially allow users to select different components or services from different vendors, to communicate between incompatible systems via networks, and to separate data from the rest of the system. (Note: In this discussion the term "interface" does not refer to user interface; it is the juncture between any two components of a system.)

It is a fallacy to state that any completely "open" systems exist. Some would argue that Unix is the exception, but Unix is an operating system, not a total system. And some flavors of Unix are actually highly proprietary. Furthermore, it is also a fallacy that open systems necessarily perform better than proprietary solutions. The outcome of such an evaluation depends entirely on the definition of "performance" (i.e., what is being tested) and exactly how it is being tested.

The notion of "proprietariness" has been much maligned. In fact, some system components function quite nicely as proprietary elements (e.g., database indexing structures or software internals). Proprietary portions of a system are the areas in which vendors are able to compete on the basis of features and performance, one of the cost factors for open systems. Whenever a vendor is required to develop a standard interface, the system at that point must perform an additional function; thus the potential for overall reduced performance is likely. If vendors have complete control of the process, however, they can optimize it in any fashion they devise.

Like most things in life, there are trade-offs with regard to open systems. Certainly having systems that can talk to one another and can share data is desirable and necessary. There are, however, areas in system design that are not required to be standards-based. Understanding and communicating these issues is a matter of intellectual honesty, not marketing hype.

Technoreligious Platform Wars

One of the most polarized issues in computing has been the question of which hardware and operating system platform to adopt. While it is sometimes possible to identify some features, functions, technologies, or applications that operate better in some environments than in others, these discussions tend to focus on perceived historical firsts, personal preferences, and unsubstantiated claims. Furthermore, they also tend to devolve into personal affronts, misrepresentation of fact, and naïveté toward contextual issues. (For example, neither Apple nor Microsoft invented the graphical user interface or the mouse; engineers and designers at Xerox PARC did.)

While it may be fun to jest about who has the most advanced technology—careful, one might be surprised by the outcome if one includes commercially unsuccessful companies—such activity may not actually serve an organization well. Organizations operate within contexts that include things such as installed base, budgetary and purchasing constraints, product requirements, support options, and technology integration. Systems librarians, indeed all librarians, would do well to focus energy on developing and getting vendors to develop cross-platform support. (A strong argument could be made that the single most influential technical component of the Internet for libraries is the issue of the potential for cross-platform support. Many vendors of operating systems, application software, and electronic resources, however, insist on structuring their products in a manner that does not truly support cross-platform use.)

The Role of Mainframes

With the ever-increasing distribution of microcomputers in businesses, organizations, and homes, many computer users have proclaimed the death of the mainframe. If mainframes could talk, perhaps they would quote Samuel Clemens, "Reports of my death are greatly exaggerated." In fact, 1997 saw a growth in the sales of mainframe solutions (Garvey 1997b). What explains this supposed anomaly in computing choices? Someone is still interested in big iron. Perhaps the exact explanation will not be known, but it is worth considering that the technological advancements that have improved the performance and reduced the costs of microcomputers and server-style midrange computers have also enhanced the value of mainframes. While the divisions between computer categories have blurred to some extent, clear differences remain in performance, reliability, appropriateness to task, and scalability among certain types of machines.

It is common knowledge that many of the tasks that used to require a large mainframe can now be accomplished on an average desktop computer. That, however, says nothing about applications that are far beyond the current crop of high-end desktop units. It is also relatively easy to demonstrate how many functions that used to require central mainframe resources can now be provided via departmental servers. Indeed, some incredibly powerful network servers support large numbers of users running sophisticated software. Any machine, however, can be overloaded at some point. And all machines, and designs of machines, have pros and cons regarding the features they provide.

From a pragmatic perspective, the most important element is the total cost to automate the function(s) adequately. At some point, a midrange server will cost as much as or more than a low-end mainframe (Schuyler 1994) and may be reaching its maximum potential (i.e., no longer scalable). To suggest that a mainframe is passé just for popularity reasons is to ignore technology needs and realities.

In the 1990s, one popular model of computing has been client-server. Many proponents of this model have attempted to bludgeon the mainframe concept to death by suggesting that distributed processing will eliminate the need for centralized big iron. What is not mentioned is that any computer, from a palmtop to a mainframe, can participate in a client-server architecture in which certain functions are handled at whatever level seems the most appropriate at which there is processing capability. It is also not frequently mentioned that applications remain, defined either by processing needs or by the total user impact, that require multiple parallel processors (e.g., in the hundreds, as opposed to the twos and threes for servers) or huge data pipes for bus traffic between processing units and peripheral devices.

In other words, there is a place for just about every size computer. The appropriateness is determined by the circumstances and the human intelligence necessary to evaluate multiple solutions. It is worth noting that the article mentioned previously states that the increase in mainframe sales is in response to failed client-server implementations, security concerns, and documented total project cost-effectiveness (Garvey 1997b).

Central versus Distributed Management

Proponents of centralized and distributed models of computing management argue that their respective ideas represent the best way to structure information technology in an organization. The centralized camp expounds on the efficiencies of economies of scale, the ease with which scarce resources can be managed, the greater security risk of placing too much access and control in the hands of users, and the value of standardization. On the other hand, the proponents of distributed models argue that keeping the technical expertise centralized discourages use of technology, large central projects and operations are inefficient by their very nature, and bureaucracy inhibits creativity and delays implementation.

The most interesting thing about this debate is that both sides are correct for the most part, even if each misses the other's points. The most important point to make is that different organizations with different histories, sizes, and personalities require different solutions. What may work well under some conditions may fail miserably under others. For example, in an organization in which departments have a long history of working interdependently on projects, a highly structured and hierarchical approach to the management of information technology may be completely unnecessary. Likewise in a smaller organization, the overhead would probably stifle any suggestion of creativity.

On the other hand, in a large organization with many departments, some units may not have the wherewithal to maintain expertise locally. Or in situations in which there has been mismanagement or a lack of trust among units, an effective central unit that services all needs may be an appropriate option. All of these examples assume that the solution at hand works. If not, then an organization needs to address the local reasons for failure.

For some proponents of either side in this debate, the real question is not what structure is most appropriate, but rather what personal experience has impressed one's mind. On the one hand, if someone has been frequently told, "No, you can't do that," or has received poor service from a central technology office, he or she may not care for that structure, wishing instead for the ability to control his or her own technological destiny. On the other hand, if someone has experienced a techno–free-for-all in which everyone is his or her own guru, perhaps some central guidance and support may seem helpful. The people who make these justifications, or others like them, in support of one approach over the other continue to miss seeing that they are dealing with failed implementations, not necessarily failed concepts. If it doesn't work, fix it, but, by all means, make sure that the entire organization is being served adequately whatever approach is selected.

The Prepositions of Technical Life

The semantics of technology are frequently ambiguous. The meaning associated with terms and phrases employed in describing processes are critical to understanding what a given technology does and does not do—and concomitantly where it is appropriately applied.

One example of this phenomenon relates to where processes run, particularly in a networked environment. Frequently, users will assume that an application runs "on" a server if they access it via a network. In some cases the process may actually be running "on" a server or host, such as with an application accessed through Telnet; in many cases, however, an application resides "at" a server, is delivered to the user "by" a network, and executes "on" the user's desktop computer. Certainly applications run "on" the server, but these are usually not user applications; they are part of the network operating system, management utilities, or network services, a portion of which executes on the server.

Another case in point is how things look as opposed to how they happen. As more services are delivered remotely through Web interfaces, increased opportunities abound to "fool" users into believing that the environment is simpler than it really is. In addition to the prepositions that describe where a process runs, the question "'To' what is a user connected?" becomes relevant. One service could be spread across several devices with some of them functioning as gateways "through" which a user passes for authentication, load balancing, or application access.

So why are these semantic issues important in technology? For users, perhaps on the surface they are merely the details of technobabble. In systems work, however, these issues are the core of understanding how something works, what avenues to pursue in resolving a problem, how to authenticate users, and which options for mapping legacy systems to new technologies will work in a given technological context. An appreciation of these subtleties will also assist a technical professional in forging through marketing hype to discover solutions that really work.

Libraries in the Age of the Ubiquitous Business Model

Libraries, as well as other institutions, in the United States have recently come under increased scrutiny for the application of business models. The idea is that through competition the organization will become more efficient. In many cases libraries are forced to justify the value of services offered and collections acquired in light of the cost of providing such things.

Many librarians come to this discussion with a set of assumptions that what libraries do is valued across the board and therefore should not be subjected to such analysis. It is unlikely that such an approach can survive much longer for most libraries. Librarians must be able to demonstrate to funding agencies (e.g., city governments, parent institutions, corporate management) in a language that those constituents understand the added value of library resources and services.

In the course of justifying continued funding for libraries, librarians need to consider areas in which operations can be streamlined, or in some cases cut. Certainly technology has been sold to libraries, and the corporate world, as a means to reduce overhead and improve service. While some technologies are relatively low-cost, high-benefit options, most applications of technology do not in fact produce immediate payoff. Up-front costs, ongoing management costs, and maintenance and upgrade costs frequently overwhelm organizations and sponsors. A more realistic approach perhaps is to view technology more as a means to maintain valuable services at predictable, slightly lower costs per unit, rather than as a fiscal messiah that will support increasing services while cutting overhead including staff.

At the same time, however, librarians must consider areas in which the application of technologies, combined with planning and appropriate discipline, can reduce duplication of effort, increase efficiency in areas that can yield some, and improve overall services to constituents. These are not new ideas, but the time has come for all librarians, including systems librarians, to devote energies to making this happen.

Vendors Know All about Computing and Networking

One of the most potentially damaging myths in systems work is the notion that vendors can be relied on to provide all information about computing and networking. For organizations that do not have any level of internal technical expertise, it is common to seek support from vendors in these areas. While many vendors offer accurate technical information, some requests for information could create conflicts of interest for vendors (i.e., they are being asked to suggest solutions in areas in which they sell products). In other cases, vendor representatives may not be familiar with certain technologies. Some organizations employ consultants to address this issue, but consultants are not necessarily free from conflicts of interest or ignorance either.

Most individuals who have been employed in systems work have stories of vendors who clearly did not understand that they were in over their heads. There are no guarantees that an organization will not get burned; even having an internal technical staff does not necessarily protect from this outcome. The best available protection comes in the form of intellectual awareness: seek information from multiple unrelated sources, ask pointed questions and demand clear answers, and never assume without some proof that a vendor understands a technology or specific application area.

Cost Per Central Processing Unit (cpu) Cycle (Moore's Law and Wilson's Corollary)

Much of the hype about the computing revolution has centered around a principle known as Moore's Law, named after Gordon Moore, one of the founders of the Intel Corporation. Moore predicted in the early 1960s that the manufacturing density of microprocessors would double every two years, thus increasing the computing capacity twofold. This prediction has been remarkably accurate over the past thirty years. There is also no indication of a decline in the rate of improvement, although at some point a theoretical maximum based on physical constraints may be reached (Cone 1997, 46). This amazing increase in the ability of a computer via its cpu to process bits of data directly led to the development of many of the objects people can afford to enjoy today: microwave ovens, cellular phones, electronic Rolodexes, motion sensors, home-entertainment centers, color copiers, boom boxes, programmable model railroads, automatic cameras, etc. In fact, even car engines are controlled by chips!

However accurate Moore's Law has been, one must not read more into it than is there. Moore's Law addresses one element of what we call a computer today—the cpu and other processing circuitry. It does not address hard drives, monitors, bus speeds, pointing devices, operating systems, software applications, network connections, or any of the other pieces that have become necessary components of a computer today. Performance and advancement in these other areas tend to follow a longer cycle of improvement. Cpu performance, or microchip capacity more generally, is critical to these advances in computing power, but taken alone, this doubling cycle can be overstated, particularly when considering expectations of what computers can accomplish in a given time frame or at a specific dollar value.

Taking this law beyond face value also ignores the recurring demand to have computers do more. Thus, just when the average cost of a middle-of-the-road model approaches mass-market affordability, it is not powerful enough to do what users want to do—or at least not so fast as they'd like it to perform! Put another way, when evaluating computing performance against cost, if an 80286-based computer or an original Macintosh alone would meet a user's computing needs in 1998, then Moore's Law would be sufficient to explain the cost savings for that level of processing. Because what users want or need to do today will not operate in those environments, however, one must invest in higher-level technology than would have been sufficient in 1984.

Let's call this Wilson's Corollary: for every jump in processor capability, there is a concomitant increase in application demand. In other words, as more power becomes available, users seek additional applications of the technology, and advancements in operating systems and software consume the expanded capability. While it remains true that the cost of computing per cpu cycle is decreasing, the cost of computing on the whole is decreasing at a far slower pace than many would suggest, primarily because of the influence of "application demand" (i.e., need for more disk space, more memory, higher video resolution, faster bus speeds, etc.). System level computing cost, as opposed to cost per cpu microprocessor, for an acceptable base configuration that is capable of appropriately running a wide array of current applications has been in the range of $2,000 to $2,500 since the early 1980s.

If only the number of microprocessors on the chip or millions of instructions per second processed by the cpu are considered in evaluating computing, one gets a skewed image of the cost. Without controlling for other influencing factors, the predictions suggest that computing power will continue to double in capability and decrease in cost every two years without end. One will conclude that computing will soon become so cheap that vendors will give away PCs. This argument begins to sound very similar to the phrase originally applied to nuclear power: "too cheap to meter."

One could argue that computers are the calculators of the 1990s for they will eventually become so inexpensive to manufacture that companies will use them as promotional giveaways. After all, the functions of early calculators selling for hundreds of dollars are available as freebies from banks to new account enrollees. This argument, however, assumes a constancy of application demand for computing (i.e., people will use computers in the same way in the future as they do today). Recent history suggests otherwise. Even if devices that have the capabilities of computers circa 1998 are given away at some point in the future, at that future time 1998 capabilities will be worth giving away.

Certainly computing power has grown tremendously, and the cost for similar processing power continues to drop at a substantial rate. The point is that total system costs are influenced by a complex set of factors that rapidly change. It is easy to get seduced into the belief that computing can be so cheap while maintaining the functionality that is needed. Given that computer life cycles in libraries are likely to be several years, systems librarians would be wise to anticipate growth in the demand for processing capabilities over time and purchase accordingly.

Computers as Capital Expenditures

Accountants and auditors establish the definition of and procedures for handling capital equipment. Examples of capital equipment are buildings, furniture, manufacturing equipment, and things with significant life spans and values that do not normally depreciate greatly over fifteen or more years. Some organizations define capital equipment according to the purchase price (e.g., anything more than

$1,000). Capital equipment in an organization usually is treated in a special fashion. It is purchased under different accounting rules, perhaps even on different accounts; it is inventoried separately; it frequently gets depreciated over a long number of years; and someone is responsible for verifying that these items are where he or she says they are.

Generally these issues do not raise concern if the capital item in question is a building or a large, heavy machine that does not move. The problem arises when an item is expensive, has a short life, and is easily moved. Computer hardware and software fit into these categories. And unfortunately computing equipment is usually considered part of the organization's capital equipment inventory. This determination carries serious implications: capital equipment must be physically trackable, have its value included on the organization's asset balance sheet, and have modifications to it that affect its value duly noted. In the case of buildings, large office furniture, and vehicle fleets, these implications seem harmless and relatively easily managed. In the case of hardware and software, however, the implications are more serious.

Certainly an organization should be able to track the physical location of each of its computers. After all, they are important and valuable investments. The challenge for hardware arises out of what value is assigned to the item, how frequently that value changes, and the actual market value of any modifications over time. Computers, even quicker than new automobiles, lose value over short periods of time, thus making it difficult to accurately reflect the item's true value. To a large degree this phenomenon has to do with the rapid pace of technological advancement and new product delivery. Wear and tear also play a role in the declining value, particularly in public computing environments. In terms of modifications to a computer, the cost of the modifications may not, in fact, increase the total value by the same amount, in the same way that renovations to a house do not necessarily pay for themselves in resale.

While it is possible to track where a particular piece of equipment resides and to update records each time it is moved, it is difficult and expensive to track software that many times functions more like a consumable (i.e., its value deteriorates over a short period of time measured in days or months, and it requires frequent replacement or upgrading). Furthermore, software doesn't really have a static physical representation—perhaps one could think of the documentation or media in this way, but not the software. This issue is increasing in complexity as more software is being distributed via the Internet and more documentation is being integrated into the software.

In addition, software is more often than not licensed rather than purchased. This fact means that an organization that treats software as capital equipment is potentially violating the terms of the agreement (i.e., in considering the item owned property). Some organizations also resell capital equipment once it has become obsolete, which would be a direct violation of most licensing agreements.

When organizations define capital equipment according to purchase price as is the case with software, the category becomes confused (i.e., it is not a piece of equipment, and it does not really have long-term value). Furthermore, the people in the organization who manage this "equipment" cannot operate efficiently, particularly when further restrictions exist regarding the maintenance, upgrading, and replacement of such equipment.

Standard accounting practice permits the depreciation of capital equipment over time. Businesses tend to depreciate computers over three to five years, while buildings might be given twenty to thirty years. An item's value goes from purchase price to zero over the depreciation period. At the end of the period it is removed from the books because it no longer has value to be calculated, although it may remain on the inventory if not disposed.

Many public institutions have not yet adopted this accounting practice for computers. Some depreciate computers similarly to other office equipment (e.g., fifteen years); others do not depreciate them at all. Unfortunately what many people may not realize is that keeping an old device on the books and on the inventory, even if it is no longer in use, misrepresents an organization's assets and costs staff time, and therefore money. Some organizations require special treatment of capital equipment both on the purchasing end and on the retirement end. A capital equipment designation can mean a delay in approval or a denial of right to dispose prior to full depreciation of the item in question.

Librarians may not embrace the idea of obsoleting computers every three to five years and software by the month. After all, they still boot up and run. This truth, however, must be balanced against the real cost of ownership and the inability to run current releases of software. Again, hidden costs are associated with using and maintaining outdated equipment. (See Chapter 5, "Technical Management," "Purchasing and Total Cost Analysis.")

While the situation is not likely to change satisfactorily in the short-term, one improvement would be to depreciate computer hardware and software on an accelerated schedule; some organizations already do this. A three-year depreciation schedule for most desktop hardware and software seems to make sense given current technology cycles and usage patterns. This approach would mean that after three years these items would have "used up" their capital value. It does not mean that an organization must dispose of them; it simply means that they no longer carry the significant value or distinction they once did for the organization. Such an approach more accurately represents the market value for this type of equipment and reduces the burden of dealing with reallocating or disposing of older equipment. Another option, perhaps even more appropriate, would be to cease designating hardware and software as capital equipment.

Librarians typically do not control accounting and auditing practices within parent organizations. They can, however, become involved in lobbying those who do with information about the implications of these inconsistent and confusing practices.

Leasing

A rising star in the financial side of computing is leasing. Many library administrators would immediately dismiss leasing options for technology, but such arrangements deserve attention. Libraries frequently lease other equipment: photocopiers, microform reader/printers, telephone systems, etc. Computers can be leased as well.

The Argument for Leasing

Leasing computers may make sense for many sites because computers have high up-front costs, high maintenance costs, and relatively short-term life spans. For example, an up-to-date desktop computer can be leased for $100 per month on a two-year contract that includes parts and labor for repair, meaning that the total cost at the end of two years is $2,400 plus tax, if relevant, and shipping. The same device costs $2,200 plus tax, if relevant, and shipping to purchase. This money, however, most likely has to come out of the capital equipment budget, which might be problematic (see the previous section, "Computers as Capital Expenditures"), while lease payments usually come out of operations. Leasing arrangements also mean that the library stays current with desktop technology because a new machine would be provided every two years when the lease is renegotiated. Discounts for large quantities also make these arrangements attractive.

In addition, most of the total system life cost (see Chapter 5, "Technical Management," "Purchasing and Total Cost Analysis") would be reduced, although not eliminated, for the library would have only relatively new equipment and it would be covered under a service agreement. Furthermore, some support may come as part of the lease contract. These factors could mean that something that if purchased would cost the library $18,200 over its four-year life span (i.e., $2,200 purchase and $4,000 per year in support), if leased might cost the library $16,800 over the same period (i.e., $4,800 lease payments and $3,000 per year in support) with the added advantage of having a replacement after two years.

The Case Against Leasing

The largest drawback with leasing is that once the payments stop or the contract ends, the equipment is removed because the library does not own it. This situation is similar to the challenge libraries face with licensing electronic resources. Leasing arrangements may also be difficult for some sites because of a lack of local suppliers for the equipment and support.

Leasing may not be a comfortable option for some libraries, but it is worth investigating for many, as it may either save money or permit the use of other types of money in the budget for IT expenditures. With regard to the argument about not owning the equipment, as mentioned earlier, libraries are already leasing other types of equipment. In addition, the value of a purchased computer after a period of time equivalent to a typical leasing contract (i.e., what a library would own) is questionable. Furthermore, library administrators need to recognize that IT, whether leased or purchased, is not solely a one-time or sporadic expenditure. IT represents an ongoing fiscal commitment for any organization that wishes to continue to reap the benefits of automation.

Maintenance Contracts

As computers have become more common in offices and homes, individuals have had the opportunity to discover the complexities of maintaining and upgrading hardware and software. Many companies over the years have attempted to sell maintenance contracts to individual users, much like the appliance store representatives selling ones for washers or driers. For many user situations, these contracts are not worth their cost. The popular computing press and consumer groups have strongly discouraged such additional investments for individual users.

Unfortunately, some have carried this negative idea over to organizational computing resources, suggesting that maintenance contracts are a waste of dollars. Some suggest buying quality hardware from the beginning, investing in spare parts, and risking the option of unavailable equipment. This suggestion may work for individuals or perhaps very small organizations, but for most institutional computing, maintenance contracts are absolutely necessary.

Hardware maintenance contracts provide for the replacement of failed equipment or parts and can include labor, advance replacement, and overnight shipment. Such contracts usually provide access to technical support or engineering staff that would be unavailable or more costly without a contract. For any mission-critical application, such service is a necessity. An appropriately negotiated contract can mean reduced operational downtime, which costs the organization real dollars, and obviates the need to second-guess what components will most likely fail. These contracts frequently include access to firmware upgrades and discounts on additional hardware.

Software, particularly large-scale applications such as integrated library system packages, can also be covered under maintenance or service contracts. In these cases, technical and application support and software upgrades are included in the deal.

Whether or not a particular contract is advantageous is a local issue, but these services should not be discounted out of hand without review. Most large organizations have some type of maintenance contracts. Depending on local human resources and budgets for repair and replacement, some technologies may best be handled locally while others are serviced under contract.

An interesting aside is that most major microcomputer manufacturers are including three-year parts and some labor in the purchase price. So whether or not an organization wishes to have a maintenance contract, it may be receiving one.

Network Computers (NCs) and the Pseudomyth of Reduced Cost

The networking industry is all aflutter with excitement for network computers (NCs). These devices are simplified microcomputers or glorified dumb terminals depending on one's perspective. They are designed to function as intelligent network nodes providing access to Web-based resources for the user while requiring less maintenance and management overhead for organizations. They boot a "light" network browser–optomized operating system designed specifically for low-level hardware. NCs are attractive for particular applications because their cost is significantly lower than a standard networked PC, and they provide enough functionality to service a variety of users.

Unfortunately, as with many new interesting and potentially useful technologies, NCs are being oversold to the market. First, the idea of a network node that is dedicated to certain functions and has limited user-configurable options is not new. There have been dumb terminals, diskless workstations, and X-terminals for many years. The difference between these older designs and NCs is that the new design is focused entirely on hypertext transfer protocol (http) delivery over a network. Thus, from one perspective, NCs are single-application devices.

Second, much of the marketing hype emphasizes the total cost of ownership of PCs—a significant investment for most organizations to be sure. Some financial factors, however, are not frequently mentioned. For example, while the up-front cost of installing PCs and the ongoing cost of maintaining them could be significantly reduced with NCs, no mention is made of the need to shift the investment toward central infrastructure for the NC model to function. The NC model assumes organization-wide networking, http interfaces for all applications that NC users may need to access, and sufficient server capacity and network bandwidth to accommodate the additional file and processing needs of this design.

Third, the economic model cited by most NC supporters assumes that organizations have already developed or purchased Web front-ends to legacy applications or http back-ends for all user applications. This assumption may or may not be true.

Fourth, NCs still must be deployed and maintained. Perhaps the potential for reduced cost in this category exists, but NCs do not zero out maintenance cost. Furthermore, because the technology is new, no reliable track records exist to indicate how well NCs have performed in terms of user expectations and support management.

These points notwithstanding, NCs may have a bright future for there is the potential in some environments to simplify device configuration. NCs may also provide another advantage: because of their low cost, they would most likely not be considered capital equipment, meaning that they could more easily be bureaucratically managed and replaced as needed. The most important aspect is that the decision to move in this technological direction requires a conscious informed process.

Computing versus Library Computing

The history of library automation is filled with examples of decisions motivated by a belief that computing in libraries is somehow different from computing in other industries. Certainly some of the largest and most complex databases in the world are library catalogs and citation, full-text, and image databases created and used in libraries. The size of some do not run in the thousands or tens of thousands of records, but in the millions of records. And the data structures are frequently mixed in type and style as well. Specialized peripherals have been created, too, such as terminals to display the American Library Association (ALA) character set and printers for book labels. So perhaps there have been some unique things about library computing that warrant thinking of it as different from "regular" computing.

In the 1960s and 1970s such thinking was justifiable because the state of computing at that time did not support flexible hardware and software interfaces. Thus, customized hardware was developed to handle specialized applications, both in libraries and elsewhere. At that time the cost of a computing implementation in a vertical market was high enough to justify the additional cost of a customized solution.

With the introduction of a greater variety of smaller computers based on integrated circuits, the market changed significantly. More options became available, and more developers could create competing products. The library community and the vendors serving it took advantage of these advances where possible, but many solutions remained proprietary in one way or another. A number of them were sold only as packaged deals of hardware and software. Even with networking, vendors and systems librarians alike preferred serial line or proprietary dedicated options for dumb terminals. Some of the hardware was designed and built specifically with libraries in mind. To be fair, other realistic options in networking did not exist until the mid-1980s.

As microcomputers and their applications began to put a different face on computing, however, significant changes occurred. The definition of library systems began to move beyond the sole centrality of the integrated library system to include other types of computing and applications. The supreme reign of the ILS in library computing had established a model of operations and philosophy—one focused on single, large-scale, proprietary, customized devices. While this approach served libraries well for the computing generation that developed it, the model continued to influence the nature of computing and networking well into the 1980s, even with microcomputers.

A good example comes from the early days of CD-ROM technology in libraries. Like Henry Ford, who said car buyers could have any color as long as it was black, most vendors would tell libraries they could use whatever hardware they wanted as long as it was IBM compatible. Supporting these products, even when local computing expertise existed, was a nightmare. Each one usually required a special configuration that was incompatible with other products. In response to this situation, many libraries dedicated workstations to one product or family of products, and some vendors started to market hardware configurations designed specifically to run their products—a solution not unlike the packaged hardware and software for an ILS.

More recently, the move to open systems and push for client-server architectures in computing have forced the gradual separation of hardware from operating system from application from network.

These developments permit an organization to make strategic decisions about changing one element within the overall "system" without changing every other component.

To some degree this move has been successful, but it has brought to light the dependence libraries created on customized solutions. Many features work wonderfully in a customized environment that appear less than thrilling in a more generic environment. The trade-off is that a more generic environment will cost less and perform better, but may have fewer features than a customized solution.

As libraries have devoted significantly more attention to staff and public computing other than the ILS, areas of computing, such as office automation, that don't have a history of or market for customized solutions have forced librarians to think in more generic terms about computing. Libraries have had to adjust to whatever the general market was providing. It is worth noting that this change has not been an easy adjustment.

Life has changed to some degree, although the struggle still continues with some products. The major thing that has changed is that librarians are now beginning to understand that there are advantages to aligning the library communities' needs, where and when appropriate, with the general products and services used by others outside libraries. There are economies of scale to be gained, and product support can be acquired from more than one source.

Libraries have taken advantage of advances in computing, but there remains a strong sense of need for the computing industry to understand "our special situation." Certainly some applications are unique, or close to unique, to libraries, but it is not at all clear that libraries ever require unique computing hardware or networks. Word processing, financial analysis, budgeting, desktop publishing, Web design, computer programming, graphic design, operating systems, and network management are no different in libraries than they are in other businesses. To argue that they are reflects poorly on librarianship.

Public Computing

Trends in Libraries

Since the mid-1980s, many libraries have installed and maintained a variety of public computing clusters. Some of these areas offered end-user online searching or CD-ROM database access; others in-cluded standard software packages for word processing, spread-sheets, and database management. With the growth in popularity of the Internet—most notably the World Wide Web—many libraries now offer access to these resources.

For years, librarians have been discussing, writing, and experi-menting with the notion of the "scholar's workstation." With the in-tegration of multiple software products and access to local and remote data, including finding aids as well as source materials all from the same computer, this goal is all but accomplished. But then again, not just yet.

Public versus Personal Computing

In the late 1970s and early 1980s as microcomputers of various types were being developed, the name given to them was personal computers, as opposed to the impersonal mainframes and mini-computers. This convention implied a familiarity and intimacy that an individual user would have with this new tool. Software was de-signed to be used for expressly personal business (e.g., word pro-cessing for letters, spreadsheets for personal budgets, and games for fun). As the technology advanced, hardware became personal-ized as well (e.g., expansion boards and peripherals could be added according to the user's wishes).

With the availability of color monitors and graphical user inter-faces, computer users were able to customize their computing envi-ronments even more. Wallpapers, autoloading utilities, software settings, and color choices all served to make the computer more a reflection of the individual user. This trend continues to this day; it even extends to networks with the ability to customize log-ins and retrieve information based on the user's interests. Individuals can create a computing environment that matches their style of working both at home and at work. This function is beneficial to the user and the organization in which the user works. Productivity and interest in discovering ways to apply the technology can increase in an envi-ronment where the user can manipulate the outcome.

In contrast to this heterogenous computing environment, li-braries also deal with expressly public computing in which there is not just one individual user. In fact, libraries remain one of the only locations, and certainly the largest, for serving up computer and database access to the general public, or defined portions of the public. This environment is challenging to manage because its essence is fundamentally at odds with the nature of personal computing. For a public setting, such as a library, it may not be appropriate for the individual user to have complete control over the environment. After all, it is not this user's "personal computer." Certain options that the user would wish to select cannot be supported for security or general management reasons. For example, the ability to save files at any location other than the floppy drive may not be appropriate on a public machine. Or attempting to change network parameters could cause a system failure and thus make the resource unavailable for other users as well.

Anyone who has worked in public computing environments, including sales floors in retail, knows that the concept of "personal computing" has influenced many users to the extent that they assume they are empowered to try anything they wish, even when it is not their computer. Options in some operating systems disable access to some functions, and separate products add levels of control not present in software or the ability to disable features not wanted. These third-party products are necessary precisely because of this tension between personal and public computing.

Trends in Public Computing

It is clear that for some things, public computing is here to stay and is growing rapidly. ATMs are probably one of the most widely used forms of public computing. While these devices currently are not customizable by users, perhaps soon that will change. The use of Smart-cards is on the rise in all types of organizations. These credit card–sized plastic cards can store small to medium amounts of information right on the card or can link to online systems that contain even more information. Many universities and businesses use them for identification and purchasing purposes. Medical records, other personal information, and financial information can be stored on them as well. Librarians may use them for identification, access control, printing and photocopying transactions, as well as circulation services.

Kiosks are appearing in a variety of locations around neighborhoods (e.g., malls, post offices, business waiting rooms, and libraries). These self-contained or networked devices provide convenient access to information on a wide range of topics and can provide interactive programs for self-service applications. As the Internet has become so popular, some cafés, restaurants, and bars have added public Internet workstations for their patrons. Companies such as Kinkos have expanded their base business of reprographics to include general public computing. These trends in public computing are likely to continue and increase. Libraries, however, will remain the primary source of licensed information resources.

Challenges

While libraries no longer can claim to be the only source of public computing, if they ever could, they can remain purveyors of the most diverse sets of information resources. Libraries provide access to not only the free resources that users can access elsewhere, but also licensed resources provided specifically for their constituents, most of whom would not pay individually for the cost of licensing these resources. Systems librarians, on behalf of the libraries and users they serve, will need to continue to install, modify, and maintain personal computers in an intensely public arena.

Be Open-Minded

Systems work entails the navigation of some intellectually stimulating and at times treacherous territory. There are many opportunities to get trapped in nonproductive thinking and to be influenced by beliefs that others purvey. The challenge for all systems people is to maintain an open mind while investigating acceptable options that address the needs of the clientele to whom they are committed.

7

The Future for Technical Professionals

They called it paradise, I don't know why; You call some place paradise, kiss it good-bye.

—The Eagles, *The Last Resort*

Technical professionals have a generally bright future. Contrary to the belief that computers are advancing at such a fast rate that support personnel will not be needed in the near future, organizations continue to invest substantial portions of their budgets in information technology support.

Support and Implementation

It is clear that computers and networks at this point in time will not install themselves, nor will they troubleshoot themselves and automatically resolve problems, nor have they become so entirely transparent that training is not needed. While it is true that the management and diagnostic tools available on the market at this time are significantly improved over those of the past decade, no sign of a slowdown appears in the use of support services. Many organizations have outsourced these services in one fashion or another, but the need has not been reduced; if anything, it has increased. The process of outsourcing a function is a matter of efficiency, not of need.

In-house training and training companies are also on the rise, suggesting that the market is far from saturated at this point. Users are not yet able to be self-sufficient in all aspects of computing and networking without some type of introduction and training; perhaps they never will be. This should come as no surprise, as users are human beings who absorb information in myriad ways and possess different learning styles.

People must experiment with new technologies of any type to understand how they might be applied to the challenges at hand. Over time as this knowledge is codified and shared, the need for ongoing experimentation diminishes. At the same time, however, new technologies arise, different problems present themselves, and new users come on board; this process is cyclical: as one technology fades, another emerges. Or as one need is addressed, others arise.

No matter what the level of technological saturation within an organization, there are identifiable cycles of exploration, experimentation, adaptation, adoption, maturation, and obsolescence. For some technologies or projects, these cycles occur at frequencies measured in hours or days; for others, the cycle frequency encompasses years. Technical professionals are involved in all phases of these cycles. Their expertise and guidance will be needed for years.

Policy

On another level, the need for technical professionals is also evident: informed, realistic public policy. Increasingly as information technology pervades society, policy issues and concerns arise. These areas of public discourse range from intellectual property regulation to information access, availability and pricing, and global economics, just to name a few. These debates and the ensuing political decisions must proceed in the light of current and emerging technologies. The process requires a realistic grasp of the technologies themselves as well as the uses and implications of them.

Technical professionals are in a prime position to inform the debate. Some concern has been expressed, as noted earlier, that the influence of technologists should be kept in check with regard to public policy. The fear is that somehow these individuals will force technology on the populace or that they will seek to control all aspects of the technology. Uninformed or misinformed public discourse, however, does not produce workable and equitable policy. Neither technologists nor "nontechnologists" have a corner on good ideas for building future communities and societies. These areas of debate are for all citizens. The focus must be based on broad participation involving both technical and nontechnical people.

Tracking on New Technology

One major challenge for technical professionals today is keeping up. The development of and change in technology occurs at a pace far more rapid than in the recent past. While this challenge can be overstated, it is becoming increasingly more difficult for people in these positions to master new technologies or new applications of technology prior to the technology itself being considered routine or retrograde in the market.

In addition, the marketplace has been reactive to these perceptions of change. Companies devote substantial resources in response to what they believe the competition is doing. Thus, if one company produces updates to existing product lines or totally new product lines at a rate faster than the user community can absorb, others will soon follow in the endless chase to arrive first to the market with a unique product. This is particularly true for consumer-oriented societies such as the United States. Technical professionals simply cannot track in great detail all possibly relevant technologies.

Be that as it may, focusing on certain sets of technological developments or applications that appear relevant may be the only survival technique in this scenario, unless, of course, one wishes to be totally consumed in the process. Along with this strategy, one must also understand that projections of what technological development will offer the world in the distant future are more the purview of science fiction than honest forecasting. On the other hand, short-term prognostications in the range of one to three years are really more like marketing plans.

Setting sights on promising technologies that may require several years of research and experimentation before mass production is profitable gives one a perspective for planning and expectation. It is important, however, to recognize whose projections are heard and to seek multiple opinions on the matter. Keep an open mind, while recognizing that no one person is blessed with the ability to see future details. The following items are presented as technologies to watch that could relate directly to library applications in one way or another:

> wall-sized flat-panel displays
>
> Light-Emitting Polymer (LEP)
>
> electronic (or digital) paper
>
> display resolutions approaching print-on-paper
>
> full-body immersion technologies
>
> subminiature, three-dimensional storage options
>
> intelligent personal digital assistants
>
> video on demand
>
> truly intelligent network agents
>
> machine learning/self-modifying machines
>
> optical computers
>
> nanotechnology
>
> sophisticated robots
>
> biochips
>
> (Hatal, Kull, and Leffmann 1997; Levin 1998;
> Spinrad 1997)

In what time frame these technologies will develop and to what degree they will directly impact libraries is certainly open to debate. They will affect a number of performance and service issues, however. As distance education and telecommuting increase, technologies that support access and manipulation of information, as well as human interaction, in manners that people find useful, and not cumbersome, will be needed—indeed demanded! As computers and networks increase in capacity and in self-configured flexibility, performance should improve. With education and entertainment venues merging and as more applications include virtual environments, the desire for three-dimensional interactions with information may grow. In interpreting the implications of technologies such as this, it is important to keep in mind that many factors influence the deployment of any development, many of them nontechnical (e.g., ability to mass-produce items, production costs, field reliability, user perceptions and readiness, legal issues, ethical issues, etc.).

Systems Librarians Specifically

So, it appears that the need for technical professionals remains at least constant and probably is increased. But what does this mean for systems librarians? Certainly they won't be unemployed, although they may not always be working in libraries. As discussed in other sections of this book, systems librarians bring to the table a vast array of skills and approaches related to technology, organizations, and information. For libraries these technical professionals offer expertise and sensibility for computing and networking within the context of a library. They share two professional backgrounds that prepare them to serve in a variety of ways. As noted previously, the need for support and implementation surely will continue, and systems librarians on the whole have a long history of fulfilling that organizational need—or managing units that provide such service.

Systems librarians, however, also provide an interface between two worlds—libraries and computing—that creates the opportunity to blend the very best that each has to offer. Libraries and other organizations would do well to consider the value of having people employed in strategic positions who understand and can communicate issues related to knowledge management (i.e., creation, organization, presentation, and delivery) and technology management (i.e., process, means, priorities, and planning).

Major Challenges in Technical Work

Despite the positive outlook for employment in information technology fields, technical work faces serious challenges.

Planning

One of the consequences of the pace of change in this industry is that planning becomes a joke for many organizations. Yes, they have a strategic document, but it doesn't, and cannot, carry any serious weight in decision making precisely because it is not humanly possible to predict trends accurately for the distant future. Many companies would go out of business if they were forced to follow plans that were developed five or ten years ago. Furthermore, few, if any, companies, much less libraries, can completely replace their investments in information technology every few years just because there is a faster processor or newer versions of a compiler, assuming they can even guess what options will provide the best return on their investment.

Budgeting

Along with planning comes budgeting. In libraries, many dislike the nature of information technology spending: it never goes down. Once an organization takes the plunge, the costs are at best stable, and usually they go up if an honest analysis is conducted of all related expenses. Realistically, however, libraries should be looking at replacement schedules of three to five years for desktop computers and peripherals and four to six years for server and host computers. These are average figures that may need to be addressed on a case-by-case basis considering the necessary performance that is demanded for a particular technology. This means that a library that has fifty computers in use should purchase at least ten replacement computers each year, and should retire ten units. In this case, approximately $20,000 should be budgeted just for replacement machines, not including service calls, spare parts, service contracts, software, or new technology. If the library wished to increase its number of available computers, then more money would need to be budgeted. Clearly most libraries see themselves not in a position to budget in this fashion. If they don't, however, they will continually be placed in a position requiring special funding for replacement technology, which is increasingly difficult to obtain. Special funding initiatives are frequently reserved for new technologies or demonstration projects.

Communication

Technical professionals historically have not been known for their interpersonal communication abilities. This circumstance must change. As libraries are increasingly intertwined with information technology, the people who understand the capabilities, implications, and limitations of the technology must be able and ready to articulate library concerns in a meaningful fashion to administrators, constituencies, and the computing industry. In addition, people in these positions must garner the support of other people in their organizations to work toward common goals. That process requires trust, and trust occurs only when there is communication.

Librarians in general also must learn to communicate their needs in a technological context. Libraries function as representatives of human communities and as such must act as advocates for those respective communities. As the technological marketplace continues to wield significant political clout, librarians must seek opportunities to inform the marketplace and the agora of the needs of the communities they represent.

Credibility

Related to communication, credibility grows out of trust. Too many technical professionals have presented unrealistic technology goals, misrepresented the complexity of technical projects, and discounted the concerns of less technically literate people. To become believable one must demonstrate a history of accomplishments in a given area. It is not the responsibility of everyone else to bow at the feet of some technical guru.

Continuing Development

For any technical professionals, or organization that employs them, to advance, sufficient investments must be made in training and development. Personal and corporate dollars are needed more than ever for technical professionals to remain educated about emerging technologies, new applications, new challenges, new options for old problems, and technological implications, among others. Furthermore, introductory material is insufficient; advanced training opportunities must be provided and funded.

The excuse that well-trained staff will only seek employment elsewhere, however true, must be dropped. While the administrative frustration inherent in such a comment is easy to understand, holding to the position only causes one to appear ineffective—even ignorant. An organization simply cannot function without trained employees. Furthermore, employees, trained or untrained, are always free to leave, and ones with high-tech skills are in high demand (Carvell 1996; Neuborne 1997; Thyfault 1996). Perhaps a more appropriate administrative focus would be to seek opportunities to build trust and incentives as a work community. It is also worth noting that in today's employment scene, companies are just as guilty, if not more so, of a lack of loyalty.

Public Computing

As noted in Chapter 6, a large portion of the computing industry is defined around the notion of personal computing. Libraries deal with personal *and* public computing, two very different beasts. This challenge will continue because public computing does not constitute a significant portion of the computer market. Fortunately, a number of tools have been developed by companies that serve this segment of the industry.

Security

Perhaps security is one of the weakest links in the library community's computer chain. Surprisingly, the very libraries that stand ready to defend a patron's right to privacy also may not be using appropriate protections for that data (e.g., unguessable passwords that must be changed periodically, limited and controlled access, etc.). To some degree security is a training issue; many people simply do not understand what security is, much less why it is important. It is a significant challenge for all systems librarians.

Access

Access issues take on two fronts: interface and authentication. The interface components of access are not what most people might think on the surface: uniform user interfaces. In this case, interface means the method and protocol of access. With the meteoric rise in popularity of the Internet, particularly the World Wide Web or http, most data vendors have or are attempting to make their products available through this means. Despite the open architecture of this environment, vendors continue to add proprietary elements to their products in the name of added value. This creates additional challenges for technical staff to resolve, and the circumstance is not helped by libraries that simply accept what a vendor does. Libraries must work together in the market to influence the adoption of more open services that offer multiple-access interface options.

Increasingly libraries must provide good-faith efforts to verify user identity in a network prior to granting access to specific resources. As more databases and other electronic resources are licensed by libraries, this need will expand. In an authentication system, identifiers are used to ensure that the users are who they say that they are and that they are in fact eligible to use the resource at that time. Authentication may also be required for access to other types of security-sensitive information (e.g., patron data, internal documents, etc.) or to determine the level of rights one has in dealing with the information (i.e., view, change, delete, etc.).

The most common mechanism used in libraries at this time for public access is the patron bar code, but there are other means. Increasingly libraries must integrate with authentication systems in place in their parent organizations. In libraries these systems tend to be relatively loose so that anyone with a user's bar code or other identifying number would be able to access the resources. Filtered network addresses (e.g., Internet Protocol [IP] address ranges), logins and passwords, and socket or port numbers are also commonly used for this purpose. Database vendors and publishers, once they understand more about authentication and the weakness of their current requirements, may demand that libraries install more secure authentication options. In the future more sophisticated and flexible systems will be necessary to ensure the validity of users, to accommodate multiple network access points for legitimate users, and to protect the resources both for the licensor and the licensee.

Standards

Someone once said, "The great thing about standards is that there are so many of them." Libraries have a long history of being involved in information standards; this will likely continue. As librarians interface more with the computing industry and the major players in that industry, the challenges will increase. The computing industry does not have a long history of playing the standards game. Certainly there are some examples, but in almost every case, alternative options are chosen by some group of companies because they fit their strategic plans more closely. In other cases, the major players in this industry simply wish to be difficult because they view the market as better served by a free-for-all in which all options compete with the "best" one winning out over time. Librarians will not change that orientation in the computing industry, but they can continue to demonstrate the value of cooperative efforts particularly in terms of networking and shared resources.

Capacity and Bandwidth

Any observant individual can see that at times computers and networks run out of processing capacity and bandwidth. These challenges will continue because supply cannot meet demand, and the demand will grow. Furthermore, the cost for most organizations to provide more of either of these across the board is staggering. While the cost of computing and networking continues to drop—or so one is told—it remains difficult to get a good estimate unless the math is calculated on a case-by-case basis. Per-port network cost projections are worthless because more often than not they are based on marketing literature that does not take into account total cost scenarios. Thus, most organizations that are already networked will migrate to higher bandwidth technologies slowly over time as demonstrated need requires. Ironically, organizations that are just now beginning to network may have the advantage, as there are many high-bandwidth options on the market that did not exist just a few years ago.

The capacity and bandwidth issue is also not helped by false representations by large and small vendors in the marketplace. The Internet is, in fact, one or two steps away from meltdown at all times. Voices are heard on both sides of the issue stating how the other side misrepresents the reality. Keep in mind the AlterNIC/DNS corruption event of 1997 in which network address resolution, and therefore access, was disrupted for several days on the Internet. Suffice it to say that the Internet is at all times fragile and susceptible to failure for a variety of reasons (Gareiss 1997), as are many other technologies. Does that mean that it is totally useless? Absolutely not. Instead there needs to be some intellectual honesty about the resources provided no matter what one wants to believe.

Forecast—Partly Sunny

The future for technical professionals is bright for those who prepare themselves well and expect serious, but surmountable, challenges.

Individuals who can function in demanding environments that require vacillating focus shifts between broad and narrow issues will do well. The abilities to learn new skills quickly, adopt new paradigms gracefully, and balance competing priorities continuously will become essential. Thus, I believe the forecast to be optimism with a 100 percent chance of challenge.

Rapid change is a common prediction for all professions. The nature and rate of change is a matter for debate, but one major need that frequently goes unmentioned is the evaluation and determination of change. The focus is often on change as an event, rather than as a process in which people participate. When change is seen as a human process, the opportunities for involvement, choice, and direction are more evident. Thus, my forecast also includes excitement with a heavy dose of realism.

Survival for Systems Librarians

Job Satisfaction

Systems librarians appear to endure successfully the complex set of challenges they face in carrying out their respective duties:

> [T]he overall picture which has been built up is a positive one. Systems librarians emerge as extremely competent and hard-working individuals, not only performing a key strategic and operational role requiring many skills and abilities, but also contributing to professional affairs beyond their employing organizations. If their duties frequently place them under undue pressure, this is balanced by the stimulus and fulfillment provided by these same factors.
>
> (Muirhead 1994c, 34)

The people in these positions in part seem able to balance the stress in the position through enjoyment of the responsibilities of the position: communicating with other systems people and receiving mutual support, playing with new "toys" that need to be implemented, and sleuthing through difficult problems. Many opportunities for teaching roles can provide instant feedback from grateful "students." The image of the systems librarian as caretaker of library computing is many times also very positive.

Strategies for Success and Survival

There is no hiding the fact that systems librarianship is a demanding field. It is not, however, without reward and enjoyment. The blending of high demands and rewards in a fashion that sustains an individual for the long haul is perhaps one of the best definitions of success. For professionals who are frequently operating behind the scenes, it is important to identify strategies for accomplishing that blend.

Visible accomplishments

The self-reports from the respondents in Muirhead's survey (1993, 1994a, 1994c) indicate a high level of satisfaction. Despite this general experience, there are times when it is difficult to see the accomplishments achieved when the current circumstance appears rather dire. Systems librarians need opportunities to view outcomes and successes of the work they have performed behind the scenes. As a matter of survival strategy, each systems librarian should routinely talk with the people who use the services created and maintained, not just to receive valuable feedback, but also to accept the thanks for a job well done.

Much of the work that systems librarians perform is not only behind the scenes, but also highly abstract to an extent that it is frequently difficult to identify the portion of a project that an individual accomplished. The same is true for the resolution of many niggling computer problems that do not have identifiable closure. In cases such as these, it is worth physically visiting areas where such services are in use to see the successes in person. Such a visit can remind the individual that the work performed does matter and makes a difference in the lives of other people.

Communication and camaraderie

Communication as a required skill for systems librarians has been discussed elsewhere in this book. Here the focus is on communicating with other systems librarians or professionals involved in computing and networking. The commiserating of fellow soldiers in the computing wars is a salve beyond belief. All people employed in these activities have faced similar affronts to their technical ability, personal integrity, and mental sanity. Having a support group, as it were, of comrades provides an opportunity to air thoughts and concerns that are not appropriately voiced on home turf. Such interactions also offer an opportunity to present questions and suggest solutions for each others' problems. Shared expertise grows! These meetings can be locally arranged or even occur online in discussion groups focused on particular technologies, products, or professional interests.

Professional involvement

A related communication opportunity exists in professional associations. Many are available locally, regionally, or nationally. Some national groups have local chapters. In addition to offering camaraderie, these associations provide sources of continuing education, job placement, conference seminars, and publications. Professional involvement is a two-way street in that it provides options to receive support and to give it in return. Systems librarians tend to be very active in professional associations.

Selected Relevant Professional Associations

American Society for Information Science
8720 Georgia Avenue, Suite 501
Silver Springs, MD 20910-3602
(301)495-0900
http://www.asis.org/
asis@asis.org

Association of Computing Machinery
1515 Broadway, 17th Floor
New York, NY 10010
(212)869-7440
http://www.acm.org/

CAUSE (merging with Educom to form THETA
 [The Higher Education Technology Association])
4840 Pearl East Circle, Suite 302E
Boulder, CO 80301
(303)449-4430
http://www.cause.org/
info@cause.org

Coalition for Networked Information
21 N.W. Dupont Circle, Suite 800
Washington, DC 20036
(202)296-5098
http://www.cni.org/

Educom (merging with CAUSE to form THETA
    [The Higher Education Technology Association])
1112 16th Street, N.W.
Washington, DC 20036
(202)872-4200
http://www.educom.edu/
info@educom.edu

IEEE Computer Society
1730 Massachusetts Avenue N.W.
Washington, DC 20036
(202)371-0101
http://www.computer.org/
csinfo@computer.org

Internet Society
12020 Sunrise Valley Drive, Suite 210
Reston, VA 20191-3429
(703)648-9888
http://www.isoc.org/
isoc@isoc.org

Library and Information Technology Association
    (A Division of the American Library Association)
50 East Huron Street
Chicago, IL 60611-2795
(800)545-2433, x4270
http://www.lita.org/
lita@ala.org

In addition, state and local chapters of these and other organizations, as well as state library associations and users groups for various systems and products are likely candidates for professional involvement.

Reading the literature

One of the challenges in reading the literature of a technical field is understanding the level of ambiguity in what is or can be known. Rather than enter a philosophical discussion on the theory of knowledge, suffice it to appeal to the "Law of Controversy: Passion [is] inversely proportional to the amount of real information available" (Gordon Bernstein in Benford 1980, 135).

The first guideline is to be aware of what kind of information is likely to be included in particular publication types. Discerning such evaluative input regarding publications is a common task for many librarians, but computing publications seem to present a particular challenge. To some degree this is because many of these publications have potential conflicts of interest: for example, an industry magazine may purport to offer critical evaluations of software and hardware, but it also receives advertising dollars from the manufacturers of these products and presumably exists to promote computing. These positions can be at odds, creating a less-than-adequate source of information.

Another factor in the evaluation of information sources in computing is the "treatment comfort syndrome"—the desire to receive information in a format and at a user level that can be understood by the reader even if it is incomplete, inaccurate, or simplified beyond recognition. Nelkin (1995) identifies a number of problems in science and technology reporting that influence the type and detail of scientific information that the general public receives. These limitations in the nature of technical reporting serve as a caution to any reader of that literature.

That having been said, I am not suggesting that such publications do not have a place. The reader should approach any source of information skeptically, even if the reader is a novice in the field. It is not difficult to get published today, and a reader should question the credentials and experience of any author (including this one!).

In the computing literature, it is important for the information seeker to know up front what type of information is being sought—and by implication then what type of source would best serve the purpose. For example, if one desires information on the latest product developments and plans, many industry news-oriented publications will provide that kind of information. Increasingly, general and business news sources cover technology companies and developments as well and can provide useful news and analysis.

It is imperative, however, that such information not be considered a substitute for technical understanding and detailed technical analysis. After all, much of this type of information is fed to the news media, both general and specialized, by the companies developing and marketing certain technologies. Thus, it should be viewed with caution. The odds of it being accurate and representative in six months is only slightly better than a game of craps.

The technology news included in *The New York Times* and the *Wall Street Journal* is useful for determining what companies are developing that is likely to have mass appeal, who is now competing with whom, and the official plans for specific technologies of company chief executive officers (CEOs) and vice presidents. Occasionally these publications will include a thought piece on technological implications. This information is useful in its own right, but again it must not be a substitute for technical detail, expertise, and realism.

Another aspect of reading the computing literature centers on the challenge to present highly specialized and excruciatingly detailed, complex information in a fashion that is readable and understandable. Many publications attempt to perform this function for a lay audience. While such an approach is useful for the novice, it is to be outgrown. The goal for systems librarians is to achieve a level of technical expertise, not to remain a novice. Certainly technical cheat sheets and crib notes are helpful, even for the most experienced technical professional. The point is not that simplified publications don't have a place, but rather to recognize that systems librarians need to be able to read technical reference works and advanced texts on specific technologies with aplomb.

A particular challenge for library computing texts is a subtle implication that computing is somehow different in libraries than it is elsewhere. Various aspects of this misunderstanding are dealt with in other sections of this book. With regard to publications, it is worth noting that a number of books are written each year addressing specific technologies or technical topics applied to libraries. While some technologies may require exploration of their appropriateness in libraries or demonstration of experiments under way, too often such publications feed the misconception that technologies change when they are implemented in libraries.

A great debate exists on whether librarians should be exposed to conceptual or pragmatic materials in their preservice training and subsequent continuing education. This debate makes no sense; in fact, both approaches are needed. On the one hand, if a technical professional does not understand the concepts that went into the design of a technology or how it fits into a family of products and services, he or she cannot begin to operate effectively. On the other hand, without a pragmatic, hands-on approach, no work would be accomplished. The two are not at odds; they work hand in hand. Any professional without both is deficient. Thus, publications that address both types of approaches are needed and should be consulted.

A common theme in technology literature is the debate of issues that cannot be solved through scientific or objective analysis—technoreligious debates. It is important to understand that multiple perspectives can, in fact, be accurate. Furthermore, one can invest a substantial amount of time getting caught up in these nonproductive discussions, or reading them, without learning anything of great value. An old rag that has been revisited time and time again is the debate over the relative performance, extensibility, and manageability of Ethernet and Token Ring networking technologies. The debate over the next generation networking technologies, ATM versus Gigabit Ethernet, is just beginning. While it is useful and at times interesting to note the justifications given on either side of a debate, the point that most technologies are successfully implemented somewhere or they wouldn't generate such intense interest seems to pass unnoticed.

Technologies don't just appear; they are created to address particular concerns and then applied to other areas experimentally. They must compete in large markets or they will not become economically feasible. Market share for a particular technology grows out of the nature of the technology itself, the level of marketing invested in it, and the number of issues it is perceived by users to address. In all, it is a complex set of factors. In reading the literature, systems librarians must understand beforehand many authors may be caught in these types of debates. Matching a technology to an application or need is what is key, which requires knowing both the technology and the context.

The following materials are recommended for their content and approach. This list is nonexhaustive as such an endeavor would quickly become book-length. There are many fine publications for technical information; most are not library-related. To build a systems librarian's knowledge base, however, requires technical and nontechnical, as well as library and nonlibrary, material.

Highly Selective Recommendations

Technology in Libraries/Organizations (conceptual)

BYTE   http://www.byte.com/

CAUSE/EFFECT   http://www.cause.org/cause-effect/
cause-effect.html

Communications of the ACM   http://www.acm.org/cacm/

Educom Review   http://www.educom.edu/web/pubs/edreview.html

Information Technology and Libraries   http://www.lita.org/ital/
index.htm

JASIS   http://www.asis.org/Publications/JASIS/jasis.html

Library Hi Tech   http://www.pierianpress.com/2P.HTM

News

The New York Times   http://www.nyt.com/

USA Today   http://www.usatoday.com/

Wall Street Journal   http://www.wsj.com/

Hybrid (technology news and practical information)

Data Communications   http://www.data.com/

Edupage   To subscribe, send the command, subscribe edupage, to:
listproc@educom.unc.edu

InformationWeek   http://informationweek.com/

InformationWeek Daily   To subscribe, go to: http://informationweek.
com/iwform.htm

InfoWorld   http://www.infoworld.com/

Innovation   editors@newsscan.com

InternetWorld   http://www.internetworld.com/

LAN Times   http://www.lantimes.com/

Network Computing   http://networkcomputing.com/

Network Computing Newsletter   To subscribe, go to: http://
techweb.cmp.com/nc/forms/newsletter.html

NetworkWorld   http://www.networkworld.com/

Platform-Specific

MacWeek   http://www.macweek.com/

MacWorld   http://www.macworld.com/

PC Magazine   http://www.pcmag.com/

PCWeek   http://www.pcweek.com/

UnixWorld   http://www.unixworld.com/

Windows NT Magazine   http://www.ntmag.com/

Reviewing

Telecommunications Electronic Reviews
http://www.lita.org/ter/

Discussion Groups

SYSLIB-L
To subscribe, send the command, SUB SYSLIB-L [your name],
to: listserv@listserv.acsu.buffalo.edu

Library Oriented Lists & Electronic Serials
http://info.lib.uh.edu/liblists/liblists.htm

Usenet News
Many relevant discussion groups can be found particularly in
the comp. (e.g., comp.unix.admin), bit.listserv. (e.g., bit.listserv.
ibm-main), and alt.comp. (e.g., alt.comp.virus) listings.

Information overload

Systems librarians need to develop their own information filters—
there is too much information to process, much of it not worth the
time. "[B]e slightly suspicious of all incoming information" (Ballard
1994, 108). News groups, e-mail lists, and online journals all provide
information, but no one can cover them all. Select sources that
broaden as well as deepen understanding, develop a personal list of
ones that are most useful, and remember that one can unsubscribe
just as easily as one can subscribe.

Investing in personal and professional development

Systems librarians are required to understand and manage a wide array of technical and nontechnical issues. As discussed elsewhere in
this book, the preparatory backgrounds of systems librarians vary
greatly. And that variance is a strength. As a matter of survival, continuing to develop both breadth and depth in technical and nontechnical areas through formal and informal channels can stimulate
a new appreciation for the demands on one's resources and provide
additional skills and coping mechanisms for dealing with them.
These activities are truly an investment in self. Certainly the libraries employing systems librarians should assist in this investment, but systems librarians cannot depend solely on employers
taking the lead. Some development may be as simple and low-cost
as locating appropriate books on technical topics through interlibrary loan or offering to review technical books for a publication.
Other options may be expensive and long-term such as college degree programs.

Picking a niche

Although systems librarians often need to function in many arenas,
finding a niche in which one can develop specialized expertise can
be helpful for local needs. In addition, such expertise can be widely
recognized in the profession through the communication channels
identified previously. Many systems librarians have made substantial contributions to the profession by sharing their expertise in
these areas with others. The recognition beyond the local organization offers some encouragement (particularly if it is missing locally)
and reminds one that the profession is larger than oneself or one's
experience.

Return to fault-tolerance, resiliency, and tenacity

To survive the onslaught of systems work, a systems librarian must be able to bounce back from defeat with renewed vigor to face yet again the exact same computer problems and user questions time and time again. These are eternal! While not all days are disasters or drudgery, certainly some will occur. It is important for people in this line of work to have developed healthy personal mechanisms for dealing with overload (in all its forms), backlog, and mental meltdown. At times like these, productivity will lower, but that is not the end of the world—giving up is.

It is essential to have options at stressful times. Some may prefer to have a talking buddy, someone within the organization who can and will listen in a safe manner to defuse the frustration of the moment. Others may prefer deep-breathing exercises, aroma therapy, or meditation. Whatever the method, systems librarians need to arrange for these ahead of time, knowing that such occasions will occur.

The element of tenacity appears when, despite what might cause others to retreat, systems librarians return for more battle. This trait has led to many successes over time. It is wise, however, to recognize that tenacity can go overboard. For example, after hours of attempting to debug a Perl script, the wisest thing might be physically to leave the project for a break that will stimulate the body physically and give the mind an opportunity to deal with other pressing needs. Systems lore includes many stories of projects that went nowhere until someone left for a nap and returned later with an answer to the problem.

Life outside

Like all other avenues of work, systems librarianship can consume one's entire life; there are no built-in stopping mechanisms to the work and demands. Certainly this is not healthy and does not effectively accomplish long-term goals within an organization or an individual's life. The individual must establish clear boundaries between work and home. Having an active agenda in one's life outside of the work environment can actually enhance work performance, but technical professionals must be wary of mixing work duties with hobbies. They are at risk of falling prey to the circumstance in which computers consume work and home time because they are truly interested in them. Time away must be time away.

Humor

Perhaps the best survival mechanism is to develop a sense of humor. Rightly placed, humor can lighten anyone's load. Systems lore is filled with funny stories that relate directly to work, but humor can involve all aspects of life. Humor connects humans one-to-one through the shared experience of laughter. One of the most effective ways to connect with people outside of systems work is to demonstrate that technical people know how not to take themselves too seriously. Humor can defuse the most frustrating of circumstances.

Balancing attention to skill

Just as in any field requiring highly trained individuals, systems librarianship demands routine attention to multilayered skills. Even after years in the profession, time must be devoted to exercising basic skills to keep them honed. An accomplished soccer player practices rebound kicks, a professional musician returns to scales and studies, and a novelist writes and rewrites. Problem solving, programming, and product development all require this attention to fundamental and advanced skills.

Cultivating a skeptical mind

Much of the daily work for systems librarians can present irony and disappointment in the sense that a fix to one problem may create other difficulties, and things don't work the way they are supposed to. While subjection to this environment may create cynicism in some, maintaining a skeptical mind toward all products, services, technologies, and suggestions is a more productive option. Questioning recommendations and solutions is always wise. One may develop a negative reputation if progress is not generally perceived, but one may also avoid time-consuming and destructive projects with a keen sense of technological realism.

Seeking wealth, not riches

Systems librarians must honestly admit that they are not likely to become rich in this profession. Be that as it may, there are opportunities to earn a living income and to benefit in other than financial ways.

Knowing when to let go

In an environment that demands attention to details and accomplishments, it is easy to get caught in the trap of investing more resources in something than its organizational value warrants. Sometimes the best thing to do is to abandon a project. Ewusi-Mensah (1997, 75) outlines a number of factors involved in the cancellation of information systems projects, including project goals, project team composition, project management and control, technical know-how, technology base or infrastructure, senior management involvement, and escalating project cost and time of completion. Personal emotional investment can also be a factor in continuing with a project despite indications of a lack of progress. Systems librarians for their own sanity, as well as the good of the organization, must be ready and willing to let go of projects that have outlived their usefulness.

Managing risk

Risk is inevitable, but the level of exposure can be a conscious decision. A record of accomplishments in which participants' needs and concerns are addressed will build trust in the context of risk. At times, it may be necessary to cut the losses as noted previously. Time, whether for technical or nontechnical personnel, is money. Understanding that everyone's time is valuable is critical to managing the exposure to risk.

Another aspect of managing risk is differentiating between problems that can be solved by throwing money at them and problems that are money-insensitive (aka financial black holes). Systems librarians must know the costs and be prepared to act. Some loss is inevitable; it is the price of experimenting and learning. In those cases, it is unproductive to revisit the past endlessly; just move on. Some problems, however, cannot be addressed by pouring money into them or insisting on a technological solution. There may be other ways to fix them, or they may be unresolvable. The world is not perfect. Pick projects cautiously and wisely, as there are always more problems than resources to fix them (Durham and Kennedy 1997, 14). Systems librarians, in consultation with others, must prioritize the problems to address. The evaluation process should be based on the problem's relationship to the organization's mission; that is the ultimate litmus test.

Going for what will sell

All managers need a keen sense of what ideas and projects are likely to receive support within an organization. While some may consider this approach amoral, it may not actually be so ungrounded as thought. In many situations it is necessary to garner support to get a project off square zero. One successful method for achieving this goal is identifying common ground and areas in which the involved parties can buy into an idea—hence the notion of selling the project. Often an organization or an individual can get what is needed by being willing to accommodate the desires of other parties. Successful negotiation of these types of political environments is a highly desirable skill.

Political astuteness

Negotiating political environments also requires asking for what is wanted while knowing what is needed. Often these processes take time to bring to fruition. With a proven track record, however, much can be accomplished. One important element of this astuteness is knowing when to risk one's political capital and when it isn't worth it.

The Perks

While most of these survival mechanisms have implied the negative side of the demands of systems librarianship, that focus is simply a matter of presentation. These have been highlighted to assist those choosing the specialty in preparing for them ahead of time. There are many positive and fulfilling experiences in this field as well.

Meet interesting people

As libraries make more public use of computing, many businesses are starting to see that librarians have expertise in dealing with large-scale system and information integration projects. These projects are also happening in business and industry. On the one hand, having the business community begin to see the value and expertise of systems librarians provides additional employment opportunities; on the other hand, it also heightens the community's awareness that libraries are fairly sophisticated in terms of computing and networking, something not many outside of the library community have known.

Develop useful services

Systems librarians have the opportunity actively to develop new and useful services for patrons. While other librarians are primarily involved in the selection of new resources, systems librarians usually are responsible for making them work within a given technological context. This contribution is significant because most resources do not work as advertised. In other cases, systems librarians may design a new feature or function from the ground up. A great deal of pride and ownership comes with these projects. When the library is thanked for providing services, the systems librarian can know that he or she made it happen.

Observe a plan come to fruition

The process of developing or installing something new is frequently lengthy and involved. After days, months, or even years of labor and waiting, a project is finally complete and revealed. The presentation of a new service, feature, or system is an exciting and satisfying event for it represents the culmination of investigating, evaluating, planning, negotiating, installing, testing, tweaking, and training.

Assist others

Creating, planning, and installing are not the only steps in the life of a technology. Systems librarians have the opportunity to support others in using it as well as assisting them in finding new ways to apply technology effectively in their day-to-day responsibilities. These solvers of people's problems get a kick from helping out.

Share lightbulb experiences

Part of training and supporting users of technology is sharing the "aha" moments when a concept first makes sense. These lightbulb experiences build a bond between people. In fact, systems librarians have them, too!

Explore new technology

Systems librarians get to play! Never underestimate the value of playing with new technology. Others may see this as a frivolous waste of time, but systems librarians know better. From this playful experimentation and exploration come tomorrow's new and exciting features and services.

The art of puttering

The French have a word, *bricolage*, that describes a process of working with whatever happens to be around. In simplest terms, the word translates to "puttering," which represents very well much of what systems work entails. From another perspective, however, *bricolage* implies "constructing new things from the materials at hand" much in the way that a sculptor fashions art (Hefner 1993, 65, 179). One form of creativity for systems librarians comes when something new is crafted out of existing resources.

Stretch intellectually

Part of the exploration process is learning new tools, methods, and perspectives. At times it may challenge the participants to the point of frustration, but in the end the technology and its application is better understood.

Considered a guru

As a systems librarian's expertise, time in the field, and list of accomplishments grow, others may begin to consider him or her a guru. That moniker is well deserved for the person devoting significant effort to a specialty and demonstrating a willingness to share his or her knowledge.

Feel the power

Systems librarians have the opportunity firsthand to experience the power of computing and networking to meet needs, to automate difficult tasks, to provide useful tools, to change lives. Even though personal computing has become fairly popular, not many individuals have the chance to see a large computing operation run as it should be.

Keep the keys

There is an awesome responsibility that comes with systems librarianship: stewardship of these tremendous resources. This duty should not be viewed as a control issue, it is not. Access to huge amounts of data and power are placed in the hands of systems librarians. It is an honor to have this trust and to share these resources wisely so that all may benefit.

Change

Constant, enduring, and exciting change is ever-present in systems work. It is an environment in which no two days are likely to hold exactly the same content. For the faint of heart, it would be overwhelming, but for systems librarians, it's a rush!

So, Why Would Anyone Want to Do This?

Indeed, the balance of pros and cons, demands and perks, for systems librarians is a delicate process. Clearly this specialty is not for everyone. It does, however, provide a wonderful opportunity for many to develop and demonstrate significant technical and managerial skills. This specialty provides an ever-changing environment that many find exciting and stimulating. Over time, the expertise that one develops becomes a highly prized entity. Aptitudes, skills, and experience build that expertise that can transform into intuition, a sixth sense, toward the challenges faced in the profession. To the uninitiated it may appear magical, but those inside know the truth: "It's not flying, it's falling with style!" (Buzz Lightyear, *Toy Story*).

EPILOGUE

In this book, I have attempted to illustrate in a variety of ways the nature of systems librarianship. It is a specialty within librarianship that entails a wide array of skills and approaches to computing and networking within the context of libraries and information-based settings. It is a blending of the traditions and cultures of multiple professions, and yet it exists as an entity of its own.

Some have expressed fear that librarianship in general is undergoing its swan song as computing, electronic resources, and other professions displace the valuable intermediation and advocacy of librarians in the world today. Perhaps there is another perspective to consider. There is some indication that, with the increased access to information of various types provided through the use of computers and networks, librarians are in greater demand because of the complexity of organizing, storing, and retrieving huge amounts of data, information, and knowledge.

Librarians in general provide an appreciation of the complexity, diversity, and richness of information and human need; a variety of means to organize information and queries and support access to meaningful content; and a commitment to service for all users. To these valuable contributions, systems librarians add technical awareness and expertise, a sense of mission larger than the individual or the technology, knowledge of the importance of the work at hand, and an ongoing commitment to get the job done. A key element in all of these intellectual and physical offerings is a sense of balance that adds realism to each endeavor.

Contrary to what some may suggest, this is a great time to be a librarian and a stimulating and challenging time to be involved in

179

systems work. The road ahead is likely to be unpaved and divergent. Negotiation of these multifarious pathways will be served well by individuals working in concert to apply these skills to the tasks at hand.

Some may also question the future of libraries, and by association systems librarians, which may call into question the need for a book such as this. I have directed this text specifically at systems librarianship because I strongly believe that libraries are not likely to disappear. From another perspective, however, even if libraries morph into significantly different institutions than we currently know, systems librarians in the various roles they play offer the best of many worlds for organizations. They are trained (or should be) not only in the organization, storage, retrieval, and presentation of information, but also in the design, operation, application, and management of technology.

Given this, systems librarians provide a means of enhancing the overall support and use of technology whether or not they are employed in libraries as we know them today. The marriage of computers and information for decades now demands skilled professionals that understand at great depth both of these intellectual universes, as well as a number of the human contexts in which this relationship resides. This need is not likely to diminish any time soon, perhaps ever. Thus, a book on the preparation of systems librarians is highly relevant to the world we inhabit today.

I am indeed fortunate to have had the opportunity to participate in a most exciting period for librarianship. I have benefited from traversing a variety of pathways in pursuit of this blended profession and welcome fellow wayfarers as we continue down the road.

BIBLIOGRAPHY

Alley, Brian. 1991. "Never before in the history of libraries. . . ." In *Library Technology 1970–1990: Shaping the Library of the Future*, edited by Nancy Melin Nelson. Westport, Conn.: Meckler.

Ambrose, Stephen E. 1996. *Undaunted Courage: Meriwether Lewis, Thomas Jefferson, and the Opening of the American West*. New York: Simon & Schuster.

Ballard, Terry. 1994. "Zen in the art of troubleshooting." *American Libraries* 25(January): 108–110.

Benford, Gregory. 1980. *Timescape*. New York: Pocket Books.

Borgman, Christine L. 1997. "From acting locally to thinking globally: A brief history of library automation." *The Library Quarterly* 67(3): 215–249.

Boyce, Bert R., and Kathleen M. Heim. 1988. "The education of library systems analysts for the nineties." *Journal of Library Administration* 9(4): 69–76.

Braeg Epstein, Susan. 1991a. "Administrators of automated systems: A job description." *Library Journal* 116(15 March): 66–67.

Braeg Epstein, Susan. 1991b. "Administrators of automated systems: A survey." *Library Journal* 116(15 June): 56–57.

Buckland, Michael. 1992. *Redesigning Library Services: A Manifesto*. Chicago: American Library Association.

Budd, John M. 1990. "Salaries of automation librarians: Positions and requirements." *Journal of Library Administration* 13(1/2): 21–29.

181

Budd, John M. 1997. "A critique of customer and commodity." *College & Research Libraries* 58(4): 310–321.

Buschman, John, ed. 1993. *Critical Approaches to Information Technology in Librarianship: Foundations and Applications.* Westport, Conn.: Greenwood Press.

Cabral, Jim, and Tammy Ruth. 1997. *Networking 101.* [interactive Web site]. [cited 7 January 1998]. Available from http://www.pugettech.com/net101/.

Caldwell, Bruce, and Marianne Kolbasuk McGee. 1997. "Outsourcing backlash." *InformationWeek,* 29 September, 14–16.

Carvell, Tim. 1996. "It's a sellers' market for nerds." *Fortune,* 9 December, 31–32.

Chu, Felix T. 1990. "Evaluating the skills of the systems librarian." *Journal of Library Administration* 12(1): 91–102.

Clarke, Arthur C. 1982. *Profiles of the Future: An Inquiry into the Limits of the Possible.* London: Victor Gollancz.

Clayton, Marlene. 1992. *Managing Library Automation.* 2nd ed. London: Ashgate.

Cone, Edward. 1997. "Beyond business: The experts speak." *InformationWeek,* 21 July, 46–54.

Corbin, John. 1988. "The education of librarians in an age of information technology." *Journal of Library Administration* 9(4): 77–87.

Dalrymple, Prudence W. 1997. "The state of the schools." *American Libraries* 27(January): 31–34.

Drabenstott, Jon. 1987. "Library automation and library education." *Library Hi Tech* 5(2): 95–104.

Drake, Miriam. 1986. "Information systems design: The librarian's role." *Wilson Library Bulletin* 61(2): 18–21.

Drucker, Peter F. 1988. "The coming of the new organizations." *Harvard Business Review,* January–February, 45–53.

Dunsire, Gordon. 1994. "A life in the week. . . ." In *The Systems Librarian: The Role of the Library Systems Manager,* edited by Graeme Muirhead. London: Library Association Publishing.

Durham, Kenneth, and Bruce Kennedy. 1997. *The New High-Tech Manager: Six Rules for Success in Changing Times*. Boston: Artech House.

Edelman, Hendrik, ed. 1986. *Libraries and Information Science in the Electronic Age*. Philadelphia: ISI Press.

Ewusi-Mensah, Kweku. 1997. "Critical issues in abandoned information systems development projects." *Communications of the ACM* 40(9): 74–80.

Fisher, Roger, William Ury, and Bruce Patton. 1991. *Getting to Yes: Negotiating Agreement without Giving In*. New York: Penguin.

Fisher, Shelagh. 1994. "What's the use of systems? The role of library systems in the education of young professionals." In *The Systems Librarian: The Role of the Library Systems Manager*, edited by Graeme Muirhead. London: Library Association Publishing.

Foote, Margaret. 1997. "The systems librarian in U.S. academic libraries: A survey of announcements from college & research libraries news, 1990–1994." *College & Research Libraries* 58(6): 517–526.

Frank, Howard. 1990. "Understanding the hidden messages in what we say." *Networking Management* 8(April): 44–46.

Gareiss, Robin. 1997. "Is the Internet in trouble?" *Data Communications*, 21 September, 36–50.

Garvey, Martin J. 1997a. "Back to the middle." *InformationWeek*, 29 September, 64–71.

Garvey, Martin J. 1997b. "Mainframes bounce back." *InformationWeek*, 7 July, 14–15.

Gibbs, W. Wayt. 1997. "Taking computers to task." *Scientific American* 277(July): 82–89.

Glogoff, Stuart. 1994. "Reflections on dealing with vendors." *American Libraries* 25(April): 313–315.

Gorman, Michael. 1987. "The organization of academic libraries in the light of automation." *Advances in Library Automation and Networking* 1:151–168.

Gould, Stephen Jay. 1996. *Full House: The Spread of Excellence from Plato to Darwin*. New York: Harmony.

Grosch, Audrey N. 1995. *Library Information Technology and Networks.* New York: Marcel Dekker.

Hancock, Bill. 1989. *Network Concepts and Architectures.* Wellesley, Mass.: QED Information Sciences.

Hanson, Daniel S. 1997. *Cultivating Common Ground: Releasing the Power of Relationships at Work.* Boston: Butterworth-Heinemann.

Hatal, William E., Michael D. Kull, and Ann Leffmann. 1997. "Emerging technologies: What's ahead for 2001–2030." *The Futurist* 31(November–December): 20–25.

Hatcher, Karen A. 1995. "The role of the systems librarian/administrator: A report of the survey." *Library Administration & Management* 9(2): 106–109.

Hawryszkiewycz, Igor. 1997. *Designing the Networked Enterprise.* Boston: Artech House.

Head, John W., and Gerald B. McCabe, eds. 1993. *Insider's Guide to Library Automation: Essays of Practical Experience.* Westport, Conn.: Greenwood.

Hefner, Philip. 1993. *The Human Factor: Evolution, Culture, and Religion.* Minneapolis: Fortress.

Henderson, Kathryn Luther. 1983. "The new technology and competencies for 'the most typical of the activities of libraries': Technical services." In *Professional Competencies—Technology and the Librarian,* edited by Linda C. Smith. Champaign: University of Illinois, Graduate School of Library and Information Science.

Hobrock, Brice G., ed. 1992. *Library Management in the Information Technology Environment . . . Issues, Policies, and Practice for Administrators.* New York: Haworth.

Jaffe, Lee. 1991. "The future of the online catalog: Who decides?" *Online* 15(January): 7–9.

Jenkins, Darrell L. 1981. "Do you want to be a systems or planning librarian? Or management analyst in an academic library?" In *The Information Community: An Alliance for Progress,* edited by Lois F. Lunin, Madeline Henderson, and Harold Wooster. Proceedings of the 44th ASIS Annual Meeting, October 25–30, 1981. White Plains, N.Y.: Knowledge Industry.

Kent, Allen. 1986. "Let the chips fall where they may." In *Libraries and Information Science in the Electronic Age,* edited by Hendrik Edelman. Philadelphia: ISI Press.

Lancaster, F. W., and Beth Sandore. 1997. *Technology and Management in Library and Information Services*. Champaign: University of Illinois, Graduate School of Library and Information Science.

Laudon, Kenneth C. 1995. "Ethical concepts and information technology." *Communications of the ACM* 38(12): 33–39.

Lavagnino, Merri Beth. 1997. "Networking and the role of the academic systems librarian: An evolutionary perspective." *College & Research Libraries* 58(3): 217–231.

Leonard, Barbara G. 1993. "The role of the systems librarian/administrator: A preliminary report." *Library Administration & Management* 7(2): 113–116.

Levin, Carol. 1998. "Roll-up displays." *PC Magazine* 17(6 January): 28.

Lynch, Mary Jo. 1996. *ALA Survey of Librarian Salaries 1996*. Chicago: American Library Association.

Lynch, Tim. 1994. "The many roles of an information technology section." *Library Hi Tech* 12(3): 38–43.

Maney, Kevin. 1997. "Technology—technology moving too fast? Be glad it's not the 1840s." *USA Today*, 30 January, B2.

Marcum, Deanna B. 1997. "Transforming the curriculum; transforming the profession." *American Libraries* 27(January): 35–38.

Martin, Susan K. 1988. "The role of the systems librarian." *Journal of Library Administration* 9(4): 57–68.

McLain, John P., Danny P. Wallace, and Kathleen M. Heim. 1990. "Educating for automation: Can the library schools do the job?" *Journal of Library Administration* 13(1/2): 7–20.

Medina, Tom. 1983, Fall. "The role of the library project manager in implementing an automated circulation–online catalog system." *Journal of Library Administration* 4(3): 35–50.

Miller, Marilyn. 1996. "What to expect from library school graduates." *Information Technology and Libraries* 15(1): 45–47.

Miller, William. 1989. "Developing managerial competence for library automation." *Library Hi Tech* 7(2): 103–112.

Mitchell, Lindsay. 1994. "Systems management in the University of Limerick Library." In *The Systems Librarian: The Role of the Library Systems*

Manager, edited by Graeme Muirhead. London: Library Association Publishing.

Montague, Eleanor. 1978. "Automation and the library administrator." *Journal of Library Automation* 11(4): 313–323.

Moreland, Rachel S. 1991. "Microcomputer support: One library's plan." In *Computers in Libraries '91*, edited by Nancy Melin Nelson. Westport, Conn.: Meckler.

Muir, Scott P. 1995. *Library Systems Office Organization.* SPEC Kit #211. Washington, D.C.: ARL Office of Management Studies.

Muirhead, Graeme A. 1993. "The role of the systems librarian in libraries in the United Kingdom." *Journal of Librarianship and Information Science* 25(3): 123–135.

Muirhead, Graeme A. 1994a. "Current requirements and future prospects for systems librarians." *The Electronic Library* 12(2): 97–107.

Muirhead, Graeme A., ed. 1994b. *The Systems Librarian: The Role of the Library Systems Manager.* London: Library Association Publishing.

Muirhead, Graeme A. 1994c. "Systems librarians in the UK: The results of a survey." In *The Systems Librarian: The Role of the Library Systems Manager*, edited by Graeme Muirhead. London: Library Association Publishing.

Nelkin, Dorothy. 1995. *Selling Science: How the Press Covers Science and Technology*, rev. ed. New York: W. H. Freeman.

Nelson, Nancy Melin, ed. 1991. *Library Technology 1970–1990: Shaping the Library of the Future.* Westport, Conn.: Meckler.

Neuborne, Ellen. 1997. "Job hopping takes off: strong economy makes climate right to take risks." *USA Today*, 1 August, B1.

Oberg, Larry R., and Bill G. Kelm. 1997. "The library systems office: Are we looking for competencies or degrees?" *Library Mosaics* 8(July/August): 12–14.

Osborne, Larry N., and Margaret Nakamura. 1994. *Systems Analysis for Librarians and Information Professionals.* Englewood, Colo.: Libraries Unlimited.

Ostler, Larry J., and Therrin C. Dahlin. 1995. "Library education: Setting or rising sun?" *American Libraries* 26(July/August): 683–684.

Peters, Tom. 1992. *Liberation Management: Necessary Disorganization for the Nanosecond Nineties.* New York: Knopf.

Pitkin, Gary M., ed. 1991. *The Evolution of Library Automation: Management Issues and Future Perspectives.* Westport, Conn.: Meckler.

Rai, Arun, Ravi Patnayakuni, and Nainika Patnayakuni. 1997. "Technology investment and business performance." *Communications of the ACM* 40(7): 89–97.

Randall, William M. 1940. "The technical processes and library service." In *The Acquisition and Cataloging of Books,* edited by William M. Randall. Chicago: University of Chicago Press.

Riggs, Donald E. 1997. "Plan or be planned for: The growing significance of strategic planning." *College & Research Libraries* 58(5): 400–401.

Rogers, Frank Bradway. 1966. *Librarianship in a World of Machines.* Nashville, Tenn.: George Peabody College for Teachers.

Rush, James E. 1992. "Technology-driven resource sharing: A view of the future." *Resource Sharing & Information Networks* 8(1): 141–157.

Saffady, William. 1994. *Introduction to Automation for Librarians.* 3rd ed. Chicago: American Library Association.

Salmon, Stephen R. 1975. *Library Automation Systems.* New York: Marcel Dekker.

Schnaidt, Patricia. 1997. "Network/IS managers salary survey." *Network Computing* 8(1 February): 31.

Schuyler, Michael R. 1994. "The quest for the Son of Deep Thought." In *The Systems Librarian: The Role of the Library Systems Manager,* edited by Graeme Muirhead. London: Library Association Publishing.

Schuyler, Michael, and Elliott Swanson. 1991. *The Systems Librarian Guide to Computers.* Westport, Conn.: Meckler.

Smith, Linda C., ed. 1983. *Professional Competencies—Technology and the Librarian.* 20th Clinic on Library Applications of Data Processing, April 24–26, 1983. Champaign: University of Illinois, Graduate School of Library and Information Science.

Sobkowiak, Roger. 1987. "Human resource management: The art of directing talent." *Computerworld* 21(8 July): 17–24.

Spinrad, Robert. 1997. "Trends in information and communications technology: The impact on the networked information environment." Presentation at the Coalition for Networked Information Fall 1997 Task Force Meeting, 26–27 October, in Minneapolis, Minn.

Spurgeon, Charles. 1997. *Charles Spurgeon's Ethernet Web Site*. [interactive Web site]. [cited 7 January 1998]. Available from http://www.ots.utexas.edu/ethernet/ethernet.html.

Stevens, Norman. 1983. "Library technology: The black box syndrome." *Wilson Library Bulletin* 57(6): 475–480.

Sugnet, Chris. 1987. "Education and automation—present and future concerns." *Library Hi Tech* 5(2): 105–112.

Thyfault, Mary E. 1996. "Wide nets casts for WAN talent." *Information-Week*, 2 December, 46.

Tramdack, Philip J. 1993. "Managing the human element: The systems librarian's point of view." *Library Administration & Management* 7(4): 209–215.

Wallace, Danny P., and Bert R. Boyce. 1987. "Computer technology and interdisciplinary efforts: A discussion and model program." *Journal of Education for Library and Information Science* 27: 158–168.

Wasserman, Paul. 1965. *The Librarian and the Machine: Observations on the Application of Machines in Administration of College and University Libraries*. Detroit: Gale.

White, Frank. 1990. "The role of the automation librarian in the medium-sized library." *Canadian Library Journal* 47(4): 257–262.

White, Herbert S. 1991. "Librarians vs. computer professionals." *Library Journal* 116(15 March): 64–65.

Wittmann, Art. 1995. *Interactive Network Design Manual*. [interactive Web site]. [cited 7 January 1998]. Available from http://techweb.cmp.com/nc/netdesign/lanindex.html.

Woodsworth, Anne. 1991. *Patterns and Options for Managing Information Technology on Campus*. Chicago: American Library Association.

Wright, Keith C. 1995. *Computer-Related Technologies in Library Operations*. Aldershot, England: Gower.

Zemke, Ron. 1987. "Sociotechnical systems: Bringing people and technology together." *Training*, 24(2): 47–57.

INDEX

189

TOM WILSON is head of systems at the University of Houston Libraries, Houston, Texas. An avid proponent of eclectic thinking, Wilson has written and spoken on a variety of topics related to libraries and computing. He is the founding editor in chief of *Telecommunications Electronic Reviews* and co-editor in chief of the *Public-Access Computer Systems Review*. As a sought-after voice of technological reason, Wilson has taught and consulted on computing and networking in public, academic, and special libraries as well as in higher-education and business settings. He has been professionally active in the Library and Information Technology Association, a division of the American Library Association, since 1986.